Conflicts in Culture

# Previous Works by Sandra Harris

Irons, E. J. & Harris, S. (2007). *Challenges of NCLB*. Lanham, MD: Rowman & Little-field.

Harris, S. (2005). *Changing mindsets of educational leaders: Voices of doctoral students*. Lanham, MD: Rowman & Littlefield Education.

Harris, S., Lowery, S., Ballenger, J., & Hicks-Townes, F. (2004). *Winning women: Women leaders in education*. Lanham, MD: Scarecrow Education.

Harris, S. & Lowery, S. (2004). *Standards-based leadership: A case study book for the assistant principal*. Lanham, MD: Scarecrow Education.

Harris, S. & Lowery, S. (2003). *Standards-based leadership: A case study book for the principal*. Lanham, MD: Scarecrow Education.

Lowery, S. & Harris, S. (2003). *Standards-based leadership: A case study book for the superintendency*. Lanham, MD: Scarecrow Education.

Harris, S. & Petrie, G. (2003). *Bullying: The bullies, the victims, the bystanders*. Lanham, MD.: Scarecrow Education.

Harris, S. & Lowery, S., Eds. (2002). *A school for every child: School choice in America today*. Lanham, MD: Scarecrow Publishing.

# Conflicts in Culture

## *Strategies to Understand and Resolve the Issues*

Sandra Harris and Steve Jenkins

ROWMAN & LITTLEFIELD PUBLISHERS, INC.
Lanham • Boulder • New York • Toronto • Plymouth, UK

Published by Rowman & Littlefield Publishers, Inc.
A wholly owned subsidary of The Rowman & Littlefield Publishing Group, Inc.
4501 Forbes Boulevard, Suite 200, Lanham, Maryland 20706
www.rowman.com

10 Thornbury Road, Plymouth PL6 7PP, United Kingdom

British Library Cataloguing in Publication Information Available

**Library of Congress Cataloging-in-Publication Data**

Harris, Sandra, 1946–
Conflicts in culture : strategies to understand and resolve the issues / Sandra Harris and Steve
Jenkins.
pages cm
Includes bibliographical references.
ISBN 978-1-4758-0517-8 (cloth)—ISBN 978-1-4758-0518-5 (pbk)—ISBN 978-1-4758-0519-2
(electronic)
1. Universities and colleges—United States—Administration. 2. Education, Higher—Social aspects—United States. 3. Discrimination in education—United States. 4. Racism in education—United States. 5. Homophobia in higher education—United States. 6. Culture conflict—United States. 7.
Conflict management—United States. I. Title.
LB2341.H3245 2013
378.1'010973--dc23
2013011931

# Contents

# Foreword

In their book *Conflicts in Culture: Strategies to Understand and Resolve the Issues*, Sandra Harris and Steve Jenkins provide a valuable resource for educators serious about embracing culture and cross-cultural conflict as a normal part of people coming together in democratic societies. This volume is a hands-on, well-organized, accessible, and relevant tool that educational leaders can use to frame and reframe seemingly intractable communication issues and conflicts in ways that honor cultures as assets on which relationships and effective educational experiences can be built. The authors have produced a highly important resource for educators, educational leaders, and policy makers interested in teaching the children who are actually in our schools, rather than some mythic conception of who they might like their students to be.

Knowing and appreciating the authors' prior works, I was interested to begin my read and to learn about their conception of the cultural highway and how it might relate to the resolution of the conflicts that abide in our schools. In the preface, they make two important points that must be at the forefront of our thinking and planning as we continue to democratize our schools and society: first, changing from a white, middle-class population to a population in which children of poverty and color make up the majority is not a problem; and second, school leaders must get comfortable being uncomfortable.

Importantly, the authors present and describe culture in its broadest context. Though race, ethnicity, gender, and sexual orientation are central topics in the book, the authors broaden cultural issues to include other manifestations such as health, age, and geographical regions, demonstrating quite clearly that "culture is like the air we breathe."

The book is a veritable toolbox of strategies for educators to use in under-standing, and changing as appropriate, their own behavior. The authors make it very clear that educators who value their students and the various commu-nities they represent are in a position to increase cross-cultural communica-tion among educators and students alike. Their use of the "flight-fight-fix" perspective, overlain with knowledge of the off-ramps along the cultural highway, provides a streamlined set of tools which educators will find very useful. Furthermore, the authors' selection of vignettes and reflection/dialog-ic activities demonstrates their knowledge of and sensitivity to cultural issues in our schools. They present a perspective that views conflicts among cul-tures as opportunities for learning.

My co-authors and I have been working with Terry Cross's cultural com-petence model for over twenty years as a major resource for our work with schools and school districts. Sandra Harris and Steve Jenkins have made a significant contribution in building on Cross's work as a gift to the genera-tions.

Randall B. Lindsey
Escondido, California
Author of books on Cultural Proficiency
Professor Emeritus, California State University, Los Angeles
February 5, 2013

# Preface

The moment a little boy is concerned with which is a jay and which is a sparrow, he can no longer see the birds or hear them sing.

—Eric Berne

The latest hot topics in the culture wars are finding their way into the public schools and often become the lead story on the local news or the latest newspaper headline. Consequently, schools are increasingly becoming places where disagreements about cultural issues, often exacerbated by groups with special interests, occur. As professors of educational leadership and former teachers and administrators, we know that school leaders spend the majority of the day engaged in resolving conflicts regarding curriculum, instruction, personnel, students, parents, discipline, and community issues, just to name a few.

We have observed that much of school conflict is rooted in varying understandings of the cultural issues on the campus. In fact, when listening to the experiences of practicing superintendents, principals, counselors, central office personnel, and teachers, we have become even more certain that much of the conflict in our schools is cultural in nature.

There is even conflict over identification terms for various minority groups. For example, almost all government accountability reporting uses the term *Hispanic*, rather than *Latino* or *Mexican American*. Yet a colleague recently protested when he was identified as Hispanic, saying, "I don't hiss and I don't panic, so call me what I am: Mexican American—with an emphasis on American!" Yet, according to the Pew Research website, the preferred identification term for Latinos/Hispanics is *Hispanic* and thus this is the term used in this book (retrieved from http://www.pewhispanic.org/2012/04/04/).

Many schools in the United States and around the world are experiencing rapidly changing demographic patterns, an issue which is adding to the natural conflicts inherent in schooling. The Census Bureau reported that in 2011, Hispanics, African Americans, Asians, and other minorities accounted for 50.4 percent of births and 49.7 percent of all children under five in the United States (Cauchon & Overberg, 2012). According to the Texas Education Agency (Scharrer & Lacoste-Caputo, 2010), in the past decade, enrollment in Texas schools from low-income families increased by almost 900,000 students, so that now nearly 59 percent of all Texas students come from low-income families. Children who are English language learners jumped from 555,334 to 815,998 in that same time period.

Minority children now represent the vast majority of school enrollments in large and medium-sized Texas cities. For example, when Northern Hills Elementary School opened in San Antonio in the early 1990s, it was in a white, middle-class neighborhood. Nearly twenty years later, in 2010, 45 percent of its students are Hispanic, 10 percent are African American, and more than 60 percent are economically disadvantaged. Additionally, some public schools report student populations with such diverse backgrounds that students and their parents speak more than eighty different languages or dialects.

Similar demographic changes are occurring throughout the United States, and in other countries as well. Changing from a white, middle-class population to a population in which children of poverty and color make up the majority is not a problem. However, problems occur when school leaders and stakeholders do not have the cultural understandings necessary to resolve conflicts. Generally, individuals are uncomfortable addressing such concerns as ethnicity, race, immigration, religion, and sexual orientation. Yet these topics cannot be ignored if leaders expect school to be a place where students learn to be part of a respectful, dynamic, democratic community.

Richard Quantz (2007) pointed out that schools are made up of "individuals and groups who need to find themselves in a place where their identities" are both seen as legitimate and valued (p. 55). Therefore, he emphasized, conflict exists in these groupings, and "understanding those conflicts is one key to understanding what happens" (p. 55). Our book builds on that premise of better understanding conflicts in culture. It is the nature of a school leader's job to deal with uncomfortable cultural conflict issues, whether the conflict involves delicate issues of race or solving a disagreement between band members and football players.

Being a leader is not easy; it is frequently uncomfortable. School leaders must get comfortable being uncomfortable. Therefore, knowing how to manage conflict is critical. When conflict occurs, choices of how to resolve that conflict always have consequences. Does one choose *flight* or *fight*? Or do leaders choose to do all that they can to *fix*, and seek a win-win solution for all involved?

Leaders who have strategies for resolving conflict in their toolbox are able to embrace this position of discomfort with grace and courage. Just as important, we believe, is the knowledge that the way in which a conflict is resolved has a strong influence on the commitment and ability to strengthen cultural understandings among faculty members, students, parents, and other stakeholders.

Lindsey, Nuri Robins, and Terrell (2010) described a process of growth from cultural destructiveness to a desired goal of cultural proficiency. Acknowledging their work as a catalyst for this book, we present a continuum on the cultural highway which describes five cultural locations (Deficit, Denial, Discovery, Celebration, and Conscience) that lead to a sixth location, which we call Cultural Community.

We believe that the goal of globally focused leaders in today's schools is to lead their schools to this place of Cultural Community. The cultural highway is not necessarily progressive. In other words, one does not always start at Deficit, then move to Denial, and so on. In fact, conflict occurs because we are all likely to be at different points regarding cultural issues at different times on this journey.

Conflict resolution has the capacity to be most successful when leaders increase their understandings of where they are as individuals, and this understanding then provides insights as to where other stakeholders are on this journey toward Cultural Community. All conflict will not disappear if everyone could just get to Cultural Community; in fact, in some cases it may even escalate. However, when leaders move toward this goal and commit to leading the school family in this direction, managing cultural conflict provides the foundation and impetus for greater growth in making richer connections with others.

The purpose of this book is to help educational leaders to traverse the landscape of conflicts in culture with greater understanding, to get comfortable being uncomfortable with cultural conflict issues, and to recognize these conflicts as opportunities for personal, communal, and institutional growth, not as obstacles to avoid. Thus, the way that leaders manage cultural conflicts determines if these issues become barriers or opportunities for personal and professional growth.

# Acknowledgments

This book originated from our many conversations with educators and from our own experiences with cultural conflicts in schools. We acknowledge all of the teachers and administrators who have shared their successes and failures as they tried to bring resolution to the challenges facing them as twenty-first-century school leaders. We also acknowledge the help and support of friends and colleagues who have listened to our ideas about cultural transitions and conflict and helped refine them by participating with us in sometimes difficult conversations.

We, of course, acknowledge friends and family, far and near, who have encouraged us to share our experiences and expertise after years of conducting trainings on conflict resolution, bullying, and building socially just campus cultures. We especially appreciate those scholar-practitioners who reviewed the book and offered their endorsements; special thanks go to Randall Lindsey for his leadership in the area of cultural competence and for his foreword to this text.

With gratitude, we acknowledge Tom Koerner, vice president and publisher of the Education Division at Rowman & Littlefield Publishing Group, for his encouragement. Tom is a personal mentor and a leader in education. Thank you to assistant editor Carlie Wall and the staff at Rowman & Littlefield Education for their expertise in the final production of the book.

Finally, we acknowledge and dedicate our book to the educational leaders of today, whose wisdom and courage guide them on their journey to Cultural Community.

# Introduction

The chapters in this book are organized around three main concepts: cultural issues located on a cultural highway continuum, a framework for analyzing conflicts in culture, and conflict resolution strategies.

In chapter 1, various understandings of cultural issues are described based on their different locations on the cultural highway. In this way, readers can self-reflect to better understand where they might be located based on their beliefs and understandings of different cultural issues. This self-reflection also encourages leaders to consider where those with whom they work and other stakeholders might be on the cultural highway—*not to judge them*, but to better understand the conflicts which occur.

In chapter 2, a framework for analyzing cultural conflicts (FACC) is provided for understanding and resolving cultural conflicts. This framework helps the reader to identify the cultural nature of the conflict within the cultural highway location; to consider choices of *flight*, *fight*, or *fix* and the related consequences; to implement appropriate conflict strategies; and then to commit to continuing forward to the goal of Cultural Community.

There are many strategies and skills to resolve and manage conflict. In chapter 3, we review four conflict strategies: LIFElines, which are critical interpersonal skills; invitational theory; five styles of conflict management; and conflict mediation.

In chapters 4 through 9, the assumption is made that transformational moral leaders have a shared goal for themselves and their institutions, which is to reach Cultural Community. In each of these chapters, the FACC is used to guide the discussion of cultural conflict issues at a specific location on the cultural highway.

All of the cases discussed are based on real-life cultural conflicts experienced by school leaders. While we suggest one resolution strategy, certainly there are other possible ways to resolve these conflicts. Leaders need to consider all of the variables in their particular conflict situations. The suggestions provided in these chapters enable readers to brainstorm other creative and appropriate solutions.

At the end of each case discussion, suggested activities are presented for leaders to continue on beyond the conflict to bring themselves, stakeholders, and their institutions closer to the desired destination. As leaders better understand each of the cultural issues along the cultural highway locations in the journey toward Cultural Community, they develop greater understandings and a greater level of comfort in navigating those issues. In this way, they are able not only to work toward resolving these difficult circumstances, but to move forward on the cultural highway with greater understanding of cultural issues. Within each chapter, there are "Stop and Consider" sections for practice and discussion of the cultural conflict cases.

Stephen Covey (2004) encourages leaders to begin with the end in mind. Educators who lead in this journey with a vision toward Cultural Community move closer to achieving this destination for themselves and for their stakeholders. Thus, transformational leaders create schools that are places of true community for all students and stakeholders. So fasten your seatbelts and get comfortable being uncomfortable with cultural conflict issues . . . the journey toward Cultural Community begins.

*Chapter One*

# The Cultural Highway

He who does not travel does not know the value of men.

—Moorish proverb

Individuals are surrounded by culture. Pang (2005) writes that "culture is like the air we breathe in. It is all around us" (p. 37). Culture manifests itself in three levels: (1) language, symbols, and artifacts; (2) customs and practices; and (3) shared values, norms, beliefs (Brislin, 1993). In essence, individuals are cultural beings, shaped by the unseen and often unknown influences that create us to be who we are. Using a theater analogy, culture is the very stage on which individuals perform.

It is impossible to separate one's cultural identity from the person one becomes. One's cultural identity is created by place of birth, age, where one lives today, parents, interests, socioeconomic position, sexual identity, gender, religious affiliations, and a host of other influences. All of us are products of multiple contexts and experiences. Cushner (2003) identifies twelve attributes of culture that researchers have suggested influence teaching and learning: race, ethnicity/nationality, social class, sex/gender, health, age, geographic region, sexuality, religion, social status, language, and ability/disability.

In addition, within each of the twelve cultural attributes are mini-cultures, such as athletics, gifted and talented, the arts, level of education, and a host of others. Your cultural identity, whether you acknowledge it or not, is the lens through which you see the world. It contributes to what you value and how you see others.

If you lived on an island with individuals just like you, cultural issues would rarely lead to conflict, even though you would still have conflict. For example, if you were principal of a rural school in which all of your students were white, middle class, Protestant, and raised on farms in a rural area, you would likely have considerable agreement regarding what should be taught in the school curriculum. Thus, learning to resolve cultural conflicts would not be a high priority. However, finding such homogenous communities is almost impossible, and they are certainly not representative of reality. Instead, educators today live and work in diverse settings with people who are alike in some ways, but culturally different in other ways.

Educators have a major role to play in providing young people the knowledge and skills they will need to successfully navigate in this diverse world. Yet there are dramatic differences in teacher and student demographics with regard to ethnicity. Coopersmith (2009) reports that 84 percent of teachers are white or of European American background, while only 7 percent are African American, 7 percent are Hispanic, and 2 percent are Asian. Only 57 percent of students are white or of European American background, while 15 percent are African American, 24 percent are Hispanic, and 4 percent are Asian. This cultural demographic gap appears to be growing, as more minority students are taught by predominantly middle-class, white female teachers (Cauchon & Overberg, 2012; Coopersmith, 2009; Keigher, 2009).

As individuals become increasingly connected beyond the traditional city, county, state, and national borders, a vast and varied cultural diversity is encountered. Effective leaders share a vision for schools to be a place of belonging for all. Educational leaders must prepare themselves, their colleagues, and young people with a better understanding of culture and how to move beyond conflicts to cultural proficiency, and then how to move beyond proficiency to establish Cultural Community.

In this chapter, we present a cultural highway continuum (see figure 1.1) for educators to become more effective participants in today's global community. We describe five locations on the cultural highway journey, leading to a sixth location—Cultural Community. Remember that conflicts in culture often occur because each of us is at a different location on this journey at different times. Also remember that one need not experience each location on the highway continuum.

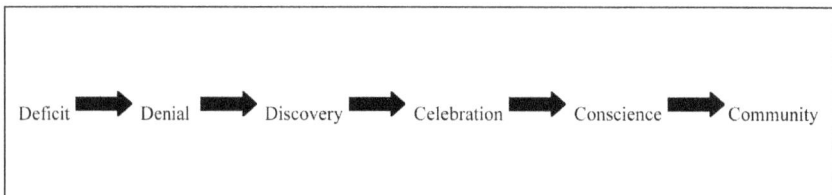

**Figure 1.1.   Cultural Highway**

## CULTURAL DEFICIT

The first stop on the cultural highway continuum is Cultural Deficit. This location is characterized by deficit and/or negative thinking. Individuals in the Cultural Deficit position view others who are different from them in a negative light. They see others as not as good as they are; consequently, their actions are discriminatory and promote prejudice, and conflicts often result. On school campuses, students in minority cultures are often excluded from activities, have no representation on the Student Council, are often not involved in enrichment classes, like AP or G/T, and are often overrepresented in Special Education.

Neither the curriculum nor the teaching staff provides appropriate role models. For example, in English Language Arts classes, such as Literature 101, there may be no evidence of Hispanic or African American literature. Stereotyping exists (e.g., all Hispanics belong to gangs, all Muslims are terrorists, all immigrants are lazy, kids from the housing project are badly behaved and poor performing, all athletes are dumb jocks, all computer people are nerds). Widespread tracking exists in the curriculum, and often ethnic minority and poverty students are tracked into vocational and low-performing classrooms (Oakes, 2005; Tyson, 2011). Expectations for students from certain backgrounds are low, or there are no expectations for achievement at all.

Conflict occurs when educators positioned at Culture Deficit make such biased comments as "These kids can't do algebra!" or announce that "these parents" are not interested in how their children achieve at school. The Cultural Deficit environment fosters bullying and other destructive behaviors when responding to students who are not "like us" (Klein, 2012). The Cultural Deficit environment communicates to others that "You are less than I am." Using a theater lighting analogy, the spotlight is on negativism or being less than.

### Stop and Consider

What are some examples that you may have observed in yourself of Cultural Deficit behavior? What are some examples of Cultural Deficit behavior that you may have observed in your school?

## CULTURAL DENIAL

The next stop on the cultural highway is Cultural Denial. Individuals at this point deny others' rights to have a different cultural identity. These individuals insist that they are "color-blind" and that they treat everyone just the same—in most cases, this means treating people like a white, middle-class

American, if living in the United States. The goal of those at Cultural Denial is assimilation, which is the "process that seeks to eliminate ethnic and linguistic practices and cultures and replace them with the host culture and language" (Pang, 2005, p. G-1).

Cultural Denial is the attitude of the proverbial melting pot; the goal is treating everyone the same. While this may sound like a reasonable place to be, it has serious implications for cultural conflict, because there are only two primary ways to treat students when individuals are at Cultural Denial. Because they say they believe in equality for everyone, the first way is to ignore different needs in order to treat everyone the same. After all, if equality is the goal, remember that *everyone must be treated the same*. This is so despite the fact that students who are from poverty, or who do not speak the language, or who are a different ethnicity than the majority, or who exhibit different talents, may have different needs. When everyone is treated just the same, there is no room for accommodations that provide special supports when needed.

The second way others might be treated when individuals are at Cultural Denial is to hold low expectations for them, which results in tracking and placing students (for example) in vocational and low-performing curricular classes. This is done not because of a belief that these students or others are "less than," as is believed in Culture Deficit. Instead, at Cultural Denial, low expectations are held as a well-intentioned acknowledgment of the circumstances in which these young people find themselves. After all, if these students, due to their circumstances, can't be expected to perform at a high level, then one is being kind to not place them where they cannot be successful.

Individuals who are positioned at Cultural Denial do not necessarily view those who are different as negative; instead, the lowered expectations reflect an attitude of what Freire (1970) termed "false generosity." One might hear teachers at Cultural Denial making comments such as "Well, their family is so poor, who could expect them to complete their homework . . . or participate . . . or study. . . ?" Consequently, less is expected of these students or individuals—all done with good intentions.

Treating everyone the same and with lowered expectations due to false generosity is often rooted in hidden biases that are never addressed. The spotlight is on being neutral or color-blind, and denying various cultural identities.

## Stop and Consider

What are some issues where you may have observed in yourself Cultural Denial behavior? What are some examples of Cultural Denial behavior on your school campus?

## CULTURAL DISCOVERY

Cultural Discovery is characterized by a discovery of cultural differences and the unique contributions that occur due to these differences. It is as though one's eyes have been opened for the first time and difference is no longer viewed as negative nor is it denied. Individuals at Cultural Discovery become aware that conflicts might occur, for example, because in some cultures a child signifies respect to a teacher by looking down rather than by looking directly into the teacher's face.

Individuals at Cultural Discovery acknowledge that some Native American cultures, for example, have a rich storytelling heritage and thus students might learn especially well from an emphasis on auditory lessons. Another example is the discovery that children from Hispanic cultures might value collaboration over competition.

A focus for behavior at Cultural Discovery is tolerance. Once differences are no longer acknowledged as deficiencies, as they were in Cultural Deficit, and are no longer ignored, as they were in Cultural Denial, this awareness at Cultural Discovery leads to the adoption of strategies to compensate for differences. An example might be an affirmative action program that seeks to level the playing field for students who come from different cultural backgrounds. Another example at Cultural Discovery is that educators recognize that teachers and administrators are often not representative of the student population; therefore, campus and district leaders make an effort to hire a more diverse, highly qualified faculty.

At Cultural Discovery, educators begin to create classrooms that accommodate the needs of children who might be different from them. However, a barrier on the road at Cultural Discovery is that educators are too frequently unsure how to meet those needs. Consequently, people continue to be stereotyped without recognition that even within cultural groupings there is much individuality (Lindsey, Nuri Robins, Terrell, & Lindsey, 2011).

Educators still fall prey to false generosity and make excuses for students who are from different cultural backgrounds, whether that cultural difference is one of poverty, race, religion, or some other factor. At Cultural Discovery the practice is generally limited to discovering and acknowledging the differences among people and the importance of *tolerating these differences*. The spotlight is on acceptance of differences.

### Stop and Consider

What are some situations in which you have engaged in Cultural Discovery behavior? What are some instances of Cultural Discovery behavior that you may have observed on your own campus?

## CULTURAL CELEBRATION

The next stop on the cultural highway is Cultural Celebration. This is an important location because here cultural differences and markers that contribute to a positive cultural identity are acknowledged and viewed as positive elements. Such events as Cinco de Mayo and Black Heritage Month are celebrated in our schools. Studies of other countries culminate in sharing ethnic foods and learning important words in those languages. Different religious holidays are acknowledged and celebrated. While not fully integrated, there is an intentional inclusion in the curriculum of literature by writers of other ethnicities and nationalities.

At Cultural Celebration, leaders recognize "acculturative stress," which is the anxiety that individuals experience when adapting to the majority culture. Thus they provide support for the emotional strain and difficulties that students of varying ethnicities face in the process of acculturating into a new society (Diller & Moule, 2005, p. 126). This is the first step toward integrating into a new and different culture. In managing cultural conflict, common ground is sought. While differences are celebrated, there is an intentional beginning to reflectively and critically examine one's own prejudices and biases inherent in stereotyping others.

On the cultural highway, Cultural Celebration is the location where the student achievement gap is confronted, not to place blame on students as in Cultural Deficit, but to identify strategies to reduce this gap. At the Cultural Celebration location on the cultural highway, the difference between equality (treating everyone the same) and equity (treating others as they need to be treated) is addressed by providing student supports, because there is an understanding that equity is more to be desired than equality. At Cultural Celebration, the spotlight is on acknowledging the value of diversity.

### Stop and Consider

What are some instances when your own behavior indicated that you were at Cultural Celebration? What are examples of Cultural Celebration that you may have observed on your own campus?

## CULTURAL CONSCIENCE

Cultural Conscience is characterized by an appreciation of other cultures and of diversity itself. At this location the goal has moved from creating a melting pot to creating a salad bowl. Educational leaders appreciate the unique differences and also acknowledge how these very differences contribute to a richer environment for all. At Cultural Conscience, educators not only examine their biases, but commit to knowing about others in a way that leads to a collaborative, collegial environment. This location could also be characterized as cultural proficiency, according to Lindsey, Nuri Robins, and Terrell (2010).

Educational leaders at Cultural Conscience begin to participate in difficult but crucial conversations about uncomfortable issues, such as sexual identity and religious differences. There is a renewed commitment to working toward equitable classrooms in which support is available to meet the needs of all students as appropriately as possible. Educators at this point on the cultural highway expect all students to achieve at the highest level possible.

Educators no longer make excuses for students who come from poverty; instead, they provide academic support through Saturday classes, extended days, and other creative scheduling possibilities. They actively seek a diverse faculty that reflects the ethnic population of the student body, when possible, and provide staff development for all that has an emphasis on cultural factors. Leaders recognize poverty as a problem not limited to schools, and where and when appropriate, they try to increase community commitment and offer support through social services.

At Cultural Conscience, leaders encourage individuals from all cultures to move toward a form of assimilation called integration, which ensures that cultural identity is maintained while creating a "new and unique third cultural form" (Diller & Moule, 2005, p. 125). Leaders integrate culturally proficient leadership throughout the school. For example, knowing and speaking multiple languages is valued and encouraged. Leaders initiate programs that support diversity. They are careful to include minority points of view in dialogue.

In essence, leaders at Cultural Conscience on the cultural highway say, "Let's join together." They emphasize collaboration to build on individual strengths and provide support for individual needs. The spotlight is on social justice.

**Stop and Consider**

When critically engaging in self-reflection, what are the cultural issues in relation to which your behavior is likely to reflect Cultural Conscience? What are some examples of Cultural Conscience that you have observed on your own campus?

## CULTURAL COMMUNITY

Too often the journey ends at Cultural Conscience, which is certainly an excellent location on the cultural highway, as leaders travel to a place where cultural conflict is lessened or indeed managed with more wisdom. However, in today's world, the journey should go beyond these cultural locations already discussed; the ultimate destination of the journey should be the sixth location, which is Cultural Community. Cultural Community is characterized by a basic respect for our common humanity. When the journey on the cultural highway reaches Cultural Community, discourse affirms all individuals, and the strengths they bring to humanity are not limited by cultural issues.

At Cultural Community, educators emphasize identifying and meeting the needs of all students and holding all students to high standards. One's knowledge of cultural issues and cultural identities becomes a useful tool in developing positive relationships with those who seem different from us, as well as those who seem like us. Leaders recognize the need for providing support for full integration into the society of the school. However, while affirming and valuing everyone's right to a cultural identity, leaders at Cultural Community move beyond focusing on the cultural qualities to instead focusing on the human qualities which we share. Regarding ethnicity, Martin Luther King Jr. spoke of this in his "I Have a Dream" speech, when he so eloquently proclaimed that he dreamed of the day when his children would "live in a nation where they will not be judged by the color of their skin, but by the content of their character" (see the King Center archives at http:// www.thekingcenter.org/archive).

At Cultural Community, work is collaborative, and everyone has a place to belong. The newest immigrant finds a place to be valued. A gay student has no fear of being bullied. The cheerleading team is diverse. A student who wears a hijab has support on a Cultural Community campus. A student who is just learning the English language is comfortable. At Cultural Community, global issues are infused into the curriculum, so that students who graduate realize that while they are American or English or Iranian or Indian, they are also a member of a world community that values humanity beyond one's cultural heritage.

Cultural Community sounds like utopia, which, of course, to some degree it is. Remember, an ideal of every leader is to commit to the very highest standard, even though they might often fall short. The writer Zora Neale Hurston wrote that her "Mama exhorted her children at every opportunity to 'jump at the sun.' We might not land on the sun, but at least we would get off the ground" (www.quotes.net). Even the motto on a US coin—*e pluribus unum*, from many come one—proclaims the goal of achieving Cultural Community.

Conflicts still occur at Cultural Community. In fact, depending on the different places where stakeholders are on the cultural highway and the issues being considered, conflict may even be exacerbated. But when leaders and other campus individuals are at Cultural Community, the strategies implemented to resolve conflicts have the potential of being at the highest level of praxis—critical reflection in action.

Throughout this chapter, a theater analogy of lighting has been used to note what the spotlight was focused on at each location on the cultural highway. In the theater different types of lighting are important. Spotlighting is important to help us focus on one particular person or action, because the lighting is so intense it causes the rest of the stage to not be visible. Thus, throughout the discussion of the first five locations on the cultural highway, the spotlight has emphasized different cultural issues at different points of time.

For example, using the spotlight, negative actions associated with Cultural Deficit were identified. At Cultural Denial, the spotlight focused on actions that were neutral, ignoring culture. The spotlight emphasized acknowledging differences at Cultural Discovery and focused on recognition of diversity and uniqueness at Cultural Celebration. At Cultural Conscience, the spotlight was on social justice actions.

Spotlighting is important to draw attention to important features at each location on the cultural highway, but sometimes the spotlight blinds the observer from seeing other areas that need attention. Rather than focusing on isolated issues, floodlighting, by contrast, emphasizes the whole stage. Floodlighting washes the stage in light and allows observers to see everything that is happening on the stage, not just one area.

Thus, at Cultural Community, the lighting changes from spotlighting to floodlighting, because this allows us to move beyond cultural issues to see the big picture and allow multiple viewpoints to be visible. With a better understanding of each of the cultural issues based on the cultural highway continuum, leaders now must look beyond the focus on cultural issues to become transformational leaders. As transformational leaders, the goal is to clearly see the entire stage and all of the players and actions that are occurring within that setting. Bennis and Goldsmith (1997) describe transformational leadership especially well:

> A leader is someone who has the capacity to create a compelling vision that takes people to a new place, and to translate that vision into action. Leaders draw other people to them by enrolling them in their vision. What leaders do is inspire people, empower them. They pull rather than push. (p. 4)

Thus, transformational leaders focus on the entire landscape of the school, where children of all cultures belong and succeed.

Leithwood and Jantzi (2005) identify three categories of transformational leadership practices in schools: setting direction, developing people, and redesigning the organization. Ultimately, these transformational leaders, who travel the cultural highway to understand and resolve conflicts in culture, have a goal to reach Cultural Community. At Cultural Community, leaders move themselves, stakeholders, and the school itself beyond the isolated aspects of culture (deficit, denial, discovery, celebration, and conscience) to view the cultural landscape in its entirety and create a much-desired community.

## Stop and Consider

What examples of your behavior illustrate Cultural Community? What are some examples of Cultural Community that you have observed on your campus?

## SUMMARY

Chapter 1 has provided descriptions of the five locations on the journey toward the sixth location, which is Cultural Community. The need for leaders to have awareness and the importance of acknowledging each of these locations have been emphasized in order to arrive at Cultural Community, where there is a universal respect for our common humanity.

## Key Thought

At Cultural Community, transformational leaders look beyond cultural conflict issues to find ways to make connections with our shared humanity.

## REFLECTION ACTIVITIES

Before you read further, use the list that follows and spend time reflecting on where you are on the cultural highway. What are your biases? What issues do you find difficult to discuss? Where do you experience cultural conflicts in your life and work? When you do this, you will be better able to resolve the cultural conflicts that occur in your own personal and professional life.

Now, reflect on where your organization is in regards to the different locations on the cultural highway. Where do the cultural conflicts occur in your institution? What are the issues that are difficult to discuss and to resolve? When you do this, you will be better able to resolve the cultural conflicts that occur on your campus.

| | **What are the conflicts?** | **How are they related to culture?** |
|---|---|---|
| Cultural Deficit | | |
| Cultural Denial | | |
| Cultural Discovery | | |
| Cultural Celebration | | |
| Cultural Conscience | | |
| Cultural Community | | |

*Chapter Two*

# A Framework for Analyzing
# Cultural Conflicts

One's destination is never a place, but a new way of seeing things.
—Henry Miller

Many school leaders are uncomfortable with conflict, and yet conflict, like change, is one of the constants in leaders' daily experiences. Too often, conflicts are left unresolved, which leads to school climates that are not conducive to learning. As leaders learn a variety of ways to solve cultural conflicts, they get comfortable with being uncomfortable and thus are able to use new skills to solve common conflicts.

The development of skills to resolve conflicts creates win-win educational environments in which all staff and students have tools to respond to any conflict, especially those cultural conflicts that exist in every classroom and on every campus. Once specific conflicts are resolved, the leader can focus on continuing the journey to influence positive cultural climate changes on the campus.

This chapter presents a framework for analyzing cultural conflicts (FACC). Remember to consider issues within the context of the cultural highway and the cultural locations that were discussed in chapter 1. Effective cultural conflict analyses can be framed using the following four steps (see figure 2.1):

1. Identify the *cultural nature of the conflict*. (What is the location on the continuum?)
2. Consider the *choices (flight, fight,* and *fix)* and *possible consequences*. (Which should I choose?)

3. Implement the *conflict strategies*. (What strategies should I implement based on my choice of *flight*, *fight*, or *fix*?)
4. *Commit to continuing on* the journey to Cultural Community. (How can I move forward?)

See appendix 1 for a form to use when working through these four steps with cultural conflict issues.

Conflicts occur every day; therefore, leaders must recognize that conflicts are a natural part of life and see them as opportunities and not as roadblocks. As Quantz (2007) points out, "conflict is normal and, while maybe not always desirable, is sometimes, perhaps even frequently, desirable" (p. 59). Consequently, educators who understand that a necessary component of leadership is to promote democratic processes also acknowledge the importance of managing some conflict through a cultural lens. Figure 2.1 demonstrates a framework for analyzing cultural conflicts (FACC), which the leader can use as a guide to analyze conflicts that occur in the journey to Cultural Community.

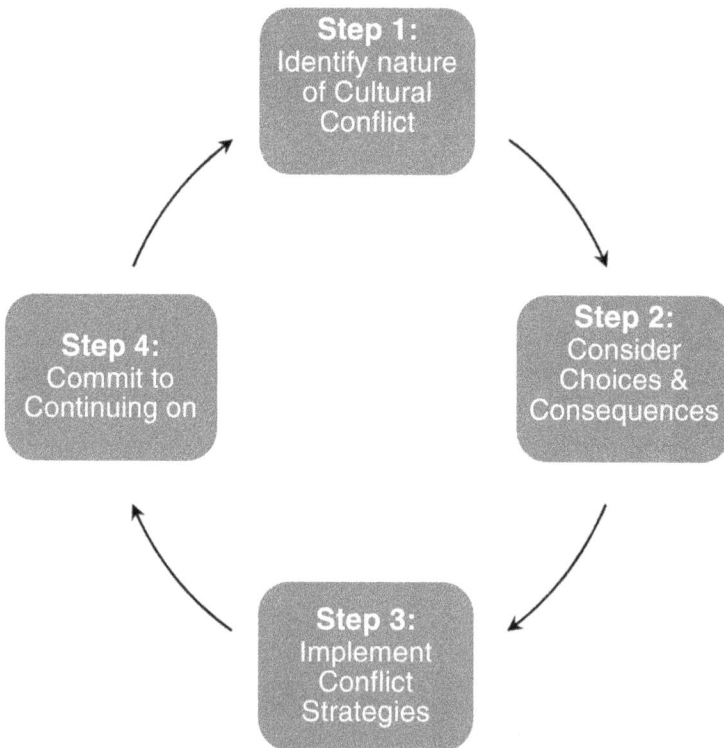

Figure 2.1.    Framework for Analyzing Cultural Conflict (FACC)

## STEP 1: IDENTIFY THE CULTURAL NATURE OF THE CONFLICT

Identifying the conflict within the cultural context according to where individuals are located on the six locations of our cultural journey is an important consideration in ultimately resolving these conflicts. Therefore, there are several questions that must be considered.

The first action is to identify the nature of the cultural conflict using the cultural locations presented in chapter 1. For example, consider the following scenario: Soon after 9/11, several students who were immigrants from the Middle East were enrolled in a school. The principal began hearing of unhappy parents who did not want their children mingling with these students. Additionally, she became aware of the students complaining that they were being harassed by other students.

In step 1 of the FACC, it is necessary to consider the cultural nature of the conflict. There are several questions which should be considered: Is the conflict a result of cultural misunderstandings? Is the conflict occurring because the individuals involved are at Cultural Deficit or Cultural Denial, for example? Are the individuals at another location on the way to Cultural Community? Or are the individuals involved at multiple locations on the cultural journey? Clearly, in this case, the conflict was located at Cultural Deficit, as the parents had negative perceptions of this culture.

### Stop and Consider

1. Do a quick review of the locations in chapter 1 that lead to Cultural Community.
2. Discuss where conflicts rooted in cultural misunderstandings might be likely to occur in your life.
3. Discuss where conflicts rooted in cultural misunderstandings might be likely to occur on your campus.

## STEP 2: CONSIDER THE CHOICES AND POSSIBLE CONSEQUENCES

After identifying the cultural nature of the conflict, leaders must consider the choices available and understand the long- and short-term *consequences* which could result. Strategies (see chapter 3) implemented based on how the leader chooses to confront the conflict will always have consequences. Choices invariably fall into one of three categories: *flight*, *fight*, and *fix* (see figure 2.1). *Flight* and *fight* are at the extreme ends of the spectrum, and there are times when these are appropriate choices to consider. However, leaders should focus much of their attention on the skills of *fixing* and resolving the conflicts.

If in the situation of the Middle Eastern students in the classroom after 9/11, the principal had chosen to ignore the problem, it is likely that soon the principal would have been faced with more angry parents, rather than the few who had at first mentioned their concern. To have chosen to fight ("I'm the principal, and you just have to accept that these kids are in your child's classroom!") was also likely to fail, especially when parents did not recognize the authority of the principal in comparison with their concern for their children. To have chosen to fix the issue would have involved several strategic conflict resolution steps that would possibly have had a lasting positive impact on the school campus.

## Flight: Avoidance Never Arrives at the Preferred Destination

Sometimes leaders choose flight as a response to conflicts. Choosing flight may make it seem like an issue has been solved at first; however, cultural conflict issues are generally not resolved this easily. Avoidance rarely, if ever, resolves the conflict. Administrators acknowledge that they avoid cultural conflicts because they are fearful of hurting someone's feelings, or because they are fearful of creating greater problems. While the initial avoidance may relieve the uncomfortable confrontation temporarily, these issues rarely go away.

Sometimes leaders choose flight when they decide to let others, who may not be suitably equipped, handle the conflict. Other times leaders might indicate "it's not my problem" and blame the conflict on the home ("It's the parents' fault.") or the larger community ("That's just how it is around here"). Unresolved conflicts with cultural issues at their heart invariably contribute to a toxic campus climate. Postponing or avoiding conflicts leads to damaging consequences. Waiting does not address the conflict, and until leaders acknowledge the conflict and take ownership of a choice to fix the conflict, it will not be effectively resolved. The consequences result in lose-lose situations for all involved in the conflict.

## Fight: Win the Battle, Lose the War

Sometimes leaders choose to fight to show their power (for example, "They will do it this way, or else!"). When leaders elect to fight over a cultural conflict, they all will likely lose the war. Fighting may take many forms. Rarely do professional educators engage in physical brawls, but these do occur.

Recently, an assistant principal shared an episode on his campus. After hearing that another teacher had told others that he was gay, the angry teacher threw open the gossiping teacher's classroom door and shouted, "If you have something to say about me, you better say it to my face and not gossip behind my back! My private life is MY private life!" Students quickly scattered as the two teachers faced off. Some of the students ran for assistance, and soon two assistant principals and a security guard came between the teachers and escorted them to the office.

Clearly these teachers had not considered the consequences when they chose to confront each other and threatened to fight over what had been heard. Both teachers were placed on immediate administrative leave, and eventually both were terminated. As administrators investigated this case, they soon discovered that rumors and prejudice had contributed to the conflict. School leaders often criticize students for not considering consequences when they explode into fighting as their response to disagreement. It is not uncommon to hear an educator say to a student when fighting has occurred, "What were you thinking?" Sadly, these two teachers failed to think and consider the consequences for themselves and for those whose lives they touched.

Fighting can also take the form of bullying or harassment and intimidation. When those in supervisory positions decide to use their power to threaten subordinates ("Do it my way, or else"), lose-lose consequences result for all involved. Victims of bullying, harassment, and intimidation can carry scars for life. So even though the old adage exists about sticks and stones, and words not hurting, words can hurt, and the harm can be severe for all parties to the fight.

### Fix: Strategies to Move Closer to the Preferred Destination

Leaders should move beyond flight and fight and instead assertively consider ways to fix or resolve the conflict. When leaders choose to do what they can to fix a conflict, resolution is more likely to occur. More importantly, when leaders choose to fix a conflict, they move themselves, others, and the school closer to the preferred destination of Cultural Community.

### Stop and Consider

1. What was the conflict when you last chose *flight*?
2. What were the short- or long-term consequences?
3. What was the conflict when you last chose *fight*?
4. What were the short- or long-term consequences?
5. What was the conflict when you last chose *fix*?
6. What were the short- or long-term consequences?
7. Since hindsight is 20/20, how might you have chosen differently for each of those conflicts, especially those *flight* and *fight* choices?

## STEP 3: IMPLEMENT APPROPRIATE CONFLICT STRATEGIES

In order to fix conflicts, leaders need a variety of strategies from which to choose. Chapter 3 describes four conflict strategy models that might be considered to bring about appropriate resolution of conflicts involving culture.

### Stop and Consider

1. Consider conflicts in general on your campus. What strategy are you most likely to implement?
2. What other strategies might help you manage conflict more appropriately?

## STEP 4: COMMIT TO CONTINUING ON

When the leader implements the first three steps, he or she identifies the cultural nature of the conflict, considers the possible choices and the short- and long-term consequences, and implements appropriate conflict management strategies. With resolution of the specific conflict, the leader can now focus on the commitment to continuing on the cultural highway journey to Cultural Community. By resolving the specific conflict, the leader is then free to turn attention to creating a community of learners engaged in continuing on in the journey.

Sergiovanni (1996) suggests that to create a community of learners requires the establishment of a covenant relationship. A covenant relationship has four components: (1) respecting and valuing diversity, (2) developing shared values and beliefs through commitment to a shared vision, (3) serving the common good by endeavoring to promote unity, and (4) supporting people to help one another achieve common purposes.

In the case of the 9/11 incident discussed earlier in this chapter, the leader identified that the conflict was rooted in Cultural Deficit (step 1). Next, the leader made the choice to fix the problem and considered the short- and long-term consequences of doing so (step 2), and then implemented appropriate conflict management strategies (step 3). The next action would be step 4, which emphasizes the commitment to continuing on to Cultural Community. To continue on, the leader works toward establishing the covenant relationship by engaging in personal critical reflection as well as involving others in conversations and activities that would ultimately lead to a greater respect for the value of diversity.

An important first step in establishing a covenant relationship with others is to provide guidelines to follow when discussing difficult or uncomfortable cultural conflict issues. Singleton and Linton (2006) suggest that these guidelines should include the following: stay engaged, expect to experience discomfort, speak your truth, and expect and accept a lack of closure. However, another agreement necessary to participating in courageous, difficult conversations is to listen to the other parties' truth. Thus, early in the cultural conversation, the leader should discuss these five guidelines with faculty and staff:

- Stay engaged—intentionally invite others to participate in cultural conversations.
- Expect to experience discomfort—get comfortable being uncomfortable.
- Speak your truth—establish a climate where everyone can speak honestly without judgment.
- Listen to their truth—commit to listening reflectively to others without judgment. Practice reflective listening; paraphrase their truth with phrases such as, "So I hear you saying . . ."
- Expect and accept a lack of closure—this is an ongoing process.

There are no silver bullets in resolving conflicts and continuing on to community. However, the purpose of establishing a covenant relationship is so that deep, critical conversations can begin to take place with leaders, faculty, students, other stakeholders, and the community. These critical conversations will nurture respectful relationships and improve understandings. At the same time, they enable the leader and others on campus to resolve conflicts while committing to continue on the cultural highway to reach Cultural Community.

## Stop and Consider

1. Why is it not enough to just solve the specific cultural conflict?
2. Why is it necessary to include commitment to continuing on as a component of the FACC?
3. Think of difficult conversations in which you might have engaged. Which of the five guidelines did you include? Which did you not include? What was the outcome? How might the outcome have been improved?

## USING THE FRAMEWORK FOR ANALYZING CULTURAL CONFLICTS (FACC)

Consider the following scenario: There is constant teasing on campus by male athletes of male non-athletes. Athletes call non-athletes names: sissy, girlie, etc. They make disparaging comments about their lack of athletic ability at every opportunity in front of others and when they are alone.

Is there a *cultural component to this conflict*? The conflict appears to be rooted in discord between two cultural groups on campus: athletes and non-athletes. The nature of the conflict appears to be located in Cultural Deficit, because the athletes are treating groups of students who appear to be non-athletic, or not interested in athletics, in a negative way. They do not value these individuals, nor do they see the strengths these individuals possess.

What choices are available and what consequences might occur? Does the leader choose *flight*, in which case he or she ignores the problem, perhaps because this is just the way this has always been in this particular community? Is it likely that the teasing issue would escalate into more serious bullying behaviors?

Does the leader choose *fight* and use his or her power to punish, even suspend, all athletes engaged in this type of negative teasing? Is it possible that the teasing would stop for a while but then resume? If the leader suspends the athletes on a game weekend, would the entire school community be angry since they might lose a game, resulting in another conflict? Or does the leader choose to *fix* the situation with a long-term consequence of improving relationships among all the students, both athletes and non-athletes?

If the leader chose *fix*, he or she would then *implement a conflict resolution strategy*. In this case, that strategy might include creating guidelines and policies at the school about how students treat others and name calling, specifically. The principal would use conflict resolution strategies that include talking with the students, both athletes and non-athletes; contacting parents; and providing counseling to reduce this cultural conflict.

How can the leader demonstrate his or her commitment to continuing on to Cultural Community? What steps should the leader take to create a community of learners committed to a covenant relationship necessary to continuing on to the destination? What could the leader do to improve the community's respect for and valuing of diversity? How could the leader develop shared values and beliefs? What actions might promote unity? How could stakeholders be supported in achieving common purposes related to the goals of Cultural Community? Perhaps the leader engaged the participants in discussing the five agreements and used these as a basis for future communication to solve cultural conflicts.

In the scenario just discussed, the FACC has been followed to identify the cultural nature of the conflict. Then choices of *flight*, *fight*, and *fix* were considered along with the short- and long-term consequences. Next, conflict resolution strategies were implemented. Last, specific steps were considered to commit to continuing on that would bring everyone closer to the goal of reaching Cultural Community.

## SUMMARY

Chapter 2 has presented a model for practitioners to use in solving cultural conflicts, called the framework for analyzing cultural conflicts (FACC). This model is based on the following steps: identifying the *cultural nature* of the conflict; considering the *choices* (*fight, flight, fix*) and understanding the *consequences* (long- and short-term); implementing *strategies* for resolving conflict; and deciding on actions that illustrate the leader's *commitment to continuing on* the cultural highway to Cultural Community.

### Key Thought

The framework for analyzing cultural conflicts (FACC) includes important steps for analyzing the cultural nature of the conflict, considering the choices and consequences, implementing conflict strategies, and committing to continuing on to reach Cultural Community.

## REFLECTION ACTIVITIES

Consider a conflict that has occurred on your campus recently. How did you decide what to do? In what way could you have used the framework for analyzing cultural conflict to bring about an appropriate solution?

*Chapter Three*

# Strategies for Resolving Conflict

Knowledge of other people's beliefs and ways of thinking must be used to build bridges, not to create conflicts.

—Kjell Magne Bondervik

There are many ways to resolve conflict, and the suggestions provided in this chapter are certainly not all inclusive, nor should they only be used with cultural conflicts. The four strategies presented here to manage conflicts when the leader chooses to work toward fixing or solving the conflict are LIFElines—critical interpersonal skills, invitational theory, five styles of conflict management, and conflict mediation. Most likely, cultural conflicts require the use of more than one strategy to fix the conflict and find a winning solution for all. Each of the approaches presented here involves guidelines and strategies to implement a process in the effort to fix the conflict.

## LIFELINE STRATEGIES

Bagin and Gallagher (2001) emphasize that certain human relations behaviors that communicate positive attitudes toward others are valuable skills in conflict resolution. They focus on the need for collegiality and goodwill among all stakeholders. Therefore, leaders must understand that communication skills involve using words and actions that are sensitive to others. The LIFEline strategies described below are communication skills that personalize the process of solving conflicts:

1. L—Learning by looking and listening
2. I—being Involved
3. F—Finding humor
4. E—being Empathetic

LIFEline skills should be embedded throughout all conflict strategies.

## L—Learning by looking and listening

Leaders must constantly be learning about the issues involved in conflict. Therefore, they must look for the big picture. They must be able to see each conflict with in-depth perception. Specifically, they must be able to make eye contact with the parties involved. An intent look focusing on the process communicates the leader's commitment to reach a mutual agreement, a resolution that is a win-win solution for all.

Leaders must also be able to read body language and nonverbal messages from those involved in the conflict. For example, crossed arms often demonstrate anger or frustration, sighing or rolling the eyes communicates distrust, and slumping in the chair indicates a lack of interest in the resolution process. Awareness of signs of nonverbal communication can help the leader make adjustments in the conflict resolution process. For example, when the leader leans forward, looks at each person prior to addressing him or her, and then smiles and nods when paraphrasing or summarizing a statement, the parties in conflict will often mirror this body language in their own communication.

Effective listening is an important way to learn. Effective listening includes active listening, which is engagement with the individuals involved and attentiveness to each statement. Another aspect of learning through listening is reflective listening, which is the skill of paraphrasing or summarizing what has been said and making sure that the summary is accurate. Effective listeners look at each individual after he or she has shared his or her side of the conflict, and say, "So I hear you saying . . . ," or "If I can summarize your side, you claim . . ." The effective listener then looks for signs affirming the summary, such as a smile or nod of agreement.

## I—being completely Involved

Leaders must be constantly involved during the conflict resolution process. As they hear and reflect on each party's side of the conflict, they need to be engaged in creating a clear and concise picture of what happened from each person's point of view. They must also be involved in creative thinking, imagining some workable solutions even before the parties are asked to brainstorm solutions. They must be able to learn from the verbal and nonverbal messages and continually adjust the process according to what is being learned as the parties work toward a solution. Involvement communicates commitment and care!

## F—Finding humor

Leaders must be able to show a sense of humor. They must be able to laugh at themselves and to laugh *with* the individuals involved, but never *at* the individuals involved in the conflict. Generally, a leader who is effective at resolving conflicts among individuals and groups must be seen as someone with a good sense of humor. Humor helps to reduce the stress that often accompanies the process of resolving conflicts.

## E—being Empathetic

Empathy is an important ability in resolving conflicts. Thus, leaders are asked to identify the feelings and the emotions emerging from the conflicts. Sometimes, just affirming the feeling (e.g., "So you are sad that . . .") will help an individual in the conflict to acknowledge his or her own emotions. A leader's understanding of emotional intelligence (Goleman, 2000) is critical in attaining an appropriate solution. Helping conflicted individuals or groups demonstrate empathy with the other is a critical step in solving the conflict.

Acknowledging and showing that one party clearly knows how the other party is feeling as a result of the conflict often begins the healing or reconciliation process. Empathetic leaders are considerate encouragers who demonstrate enthusiasm for helping others try to resolve a conflict. Empathy is the energy, initiative, and enthusiasm that conveys an attitude of *we can do this—we can get this resolved—we can all win!*

A critical skill in resolving cultural conflicts is demonstrating a commitment to the process and focusing on helping the parties solve the conflict. Leaders must be seen as neutral but must be able to demonstrate empathy (e.g., "if I were in your shoes, I would feel . . ."). This does not mean that leaders must act without emotion, because emotions are necessary to successful solutions. It does mean that the leader must not show favoritism; instead, the leader should be enthusiastic about reaching a win-win solution that will contribute to a healthy campus climate.

## Stop and Consider

1. Consider the critical interpersonal skills of LIFElines when solving conflicts.
2. Which of these do you frequently exhibit?
3. Which ones do you not exhibit?
4. What can you do to improve areas of weakness?

# INVITATIONAL THEORY

Purkey (1992) outlines an approach to conflict resolution based on four understandings: trust, respect, optimism, and intentionality. Because these four understandings are consistent with those of building covenant relationships, they are especially important in resolving cultural conflicts:

- Trust—Recognize the interdependence of all human beings and the need for mutual trust.
- Respect—Acknowledge that people have the capacity to do what is right, are valuable, and should be treated accordingly.
- Optimism—Understand that people have untapped potential in every aspect of their lives.
- Intentionality—The focus on policies and actions regarding others must be designed with intention to invite and encourage development of others.

Conflict resolution that is based on invitational theory utilizes five "C" words, and advocates employing the lowest "C" strategy first and only moving upward through the higher "C" strategies as necessary. Those strategies are concern, confer, consult, confront, and combat.

## Concern

Concern begins with the leader critically reflecting on the following questions: (1) Is this really a concern? (2) What happens if the issue is overlooked? (3) Will it resolve itself without intervention? (4) Is this the proper time to be concerned about this conflict? (5) Are resources and information available to resolve the conflict? (6) What are my own personal prejudices or biases regarding this issue? It is critical that the leader contemplate and acknowledge these issues in order to begin the first step in bringing the issue to resolution.

## Confer

Conferring as a strategy begins with an informal, private, nonthreatening, and respectful conversation with the individuals involved. Even though this is informal, the leader must be clear so that the individuals involved understand the concern and why it is a concern. The leader must clearly indicate what is needed. Compromise is often an effective strategy at this point.

## Consult

Consulting as a strategy is more formal and is employed as a follow-up when an informal conference does not result in the desired resolution to the problem, or the conflict is such that a simple information conference is not suffi-cient. In a consultation, the leader must be very clear to those involved about what is expected. Support must be provided to ensure that those involved abide by the decision. Consequences for not abiding by the appropriate deci-sion should be considered.

## Confront

Confrontation is employed when the conflict has not yet been resolved or is of such a nature that it must be dealt with more seriously. The leader should consider here whether previous efforts have been made to resolve the conflict at each of the lower levels. The leader should also be aware of the importance of documented evidence that lower strategy levels have been attempted. The leader must be sure that he or she has the authority to follow through with stated consequences.

## Combat

When the strategy needed is combat, the leader must combat the situation, not the individual(s). In other words, it is imperative that the leader focus on the issues of concern and not on the personalities involved. Do not let the "conflict battle" keep individuals from compromising to reach an agreeable situation with all parties if this is a possibility. When a leader successfully combats the issues, a consensus is often achieved in which all parties mutual-ly agree on the solutions.

## Stop and Consider

1. Identify a recent cultural conflict on your campus, or perhaps one in which you are currently engaged.
2. How could you use aspects of invitational theory to reach an appropri-ate solution?
3. Did you use any of the five "C" strategies of invitational theory?
4. If yes, which of the "C" strategies were used and why?
5. What was the outcome?

### FIVE STYLES OF CONFLICT MANAGEMENT

Based on the work of Thomas (1976), Hoy and Miskel (2001) examine five styles of conflict management related to two basic dimensions of conflict—organizational (on a continuum from assertive to unassertive) and personal (on a continuum from uncooperative to cooperative). These five styles are avoiding, compromising, competing, accommodating, and collaborating. These styles provide the following strategies for managing conflict:

1. Avoiding—This is unassertive and uncooperative. Leaders who are avoiders ignore conflict. When issues are very minor or when things just need time to "cool down," avoidance can be an effective strategy. However, when issues need to be handled immediately, avoidance can be a serious misstep. At times, avoidance can be seen as flight and not result in a fix.
2. Compromising—This style of conflict management seeks to find a middle ground. If demands on both sides are reasonable, this style requires both to make some concessions; consequently, some see this as a lose-lose situation.
3. Competing—This style is low in cooperation and high in assertiveness. Certainly, leaders must sometimes make decisions assertively; however, when used too often or in situations where cooperation is important, this can lead to greater conflict. Competing should rarely become the fight response because it often escalates into more serious conflict.
4. Accommodating—This style is highly cooperative but low in assertiveness. Accommodating is often used when a leader is trying to build support for other more important issues. However, often this strategy suggests the leader is not strongly committed to the conflict under consideration.
5. Collaborating—This is generally a win-win for all concerned. Collaboration indicates a leader who is balanced and who works well with others, and is high in both cooperation and in assertiveness. Collaborative leadership is critical to building cultural community.

**Stop and Consider**

1. Think of a recent conflict on your campus.
2. How might these five styles of conflict management have resulted in conflict resolution?

## CONFLICT MEDIATION STRATEGIES

Another strategy is conflict mediation, which employs a third party to help resolve the conflict. Many times school leaders find themselves in the role of mediator. The formal steps in conflict mediation include the following strategies, which can be implemented in isolation or in conjunction with more than one step:

1. Negotiation—Parties agree to engage in discussion with the purpose of reaching a mutual agreement. The parties are focused on solutions for the future and not on personalities or positions of authority.
2. Mediation—Parties agree to ask a neutral third party to serve as an intermediary to guide the conflicting parties to a mutual agreement. The third-party mediator does not take sides, but may help the parties consider a variety of choices and consequences to assist them in reaching an agreement satisfactory to all of the parties involved in the conflict.
3. Facilitation—Parties agree to have neutral parties lead a process designed to increase effective communication, clarify issues, consider choices and consequences, and reach consensus to resolve the conflicts.
4. Accommodation—Parties agree to adapt or adjust to differences and to focus on the reconciliation of conflicts.
5. Conciliation—Parties address existing hostilities and distrusts, and follow a process to overcome the hostilities and agree to reconcile or become compatible with one another.
6. Arbitration—Parties in conflict agree to empower a third party to determine a solution to the conflicts. The most common form of arbitration is when a judge serves as judge and jury. Often time, campus leaders find themselves having to consider arbitration as the only choice if parties are unable to work together in mediation or negotiation to reach a mutually agreed-upon solution. The parties in this case can only agree to turn the choice of solutions over to a third party, often someone in a position of authority.

See appendix 2 for a mediator report form.

## Stop and Consider

1. Of the steps in conflict mediation, which ones are you most likely to use? Why?
2. Which steps in conflict mediation are you least likely to use? Why?

## SUMMARY

In this chapter, four specific conflict approaches have been discussed: LIFElines, invitational theory, five conflict management styles, and conflict mediation. Having these processes and their related strategies available in one's toolbox will provide leaders with necessary skills when resolving cultural conflicts.

After attending a course on Conflict Resolution Skills for School Leaders, an educational leadership student drew a person from the waist up. The figure had huge ears, big eyes, and a small mouth with a smile; the arms were outstretched and open, but the figure had very thick skin; and lastly, the figure appeared to be wearing a striped shirt, like a referee's attire. The student wrote:

> Having spent the last year on my campus as the lead administrator and using all of the conflict resolution strategies [taught], I [created] this *Anatomy of a School Leader*—big ears for effective listening, engaged eyes to see all that is happening, and a small mouth to help you think before you speak but remember to have a smile because it can become contagious; and of course, thick skin so you won't get your feelings hurt easily; and finally, the referee shirt because often you are called upon to be the fairness enforcer! Feel free to share this drawing with aspiring administrators!

Sometimes a picture is worth a thousand words.

## Key Thought

The development of skills to resolve conflict creates win-win educational environments in which leaders have tools to respond to any conflict, especially cultural conflicts that exist in schools.

## REFLECTION ACTIVITIES

1. Which of the four conflict resolution strategies discussed in this chapter have you had experience using?
2. Reflect on the experience(s). Was the desired outcome achieved? Why or why not?
3. How might you handle the conflict differently today?

# Chapter Four

# First Stop on the Cultural Highway

## *Cultural Deficit*

Drying her eyes, Mother said to Totto-chan very slowly, "You're Japanese and Masao-chan comes from a country called Korea. But he's a child, just like you. So, Totto-chan, dear, don't ever think of people as different. Don't think, 'That person's a Japanese, or this person's a Korean.' Be nice to Masao-chan. It's so sad that some people think other people aren't nice just because they're Koreans."

—Tetsuko Kuroyanagi, *Totto-chan: The Little Girl at the Window*

### REMEMBER: CULTURAL DEFICIT

Remember the following about Cultural Deficit, as discussed in chapter 1:

- Cultural Deficit looks like oppression, no or low expectations, tracking, exclusion, discrimination, segregation, and negative stereotyping.
- Cultural Deficit says, "You are less than . . ."
- The practices at Cultural Deficit are destructive and prejudicial.
- The spotlight at Cultural Deficit is on negative or "less than" behaviors.

Conflict occurs at Cultural Deficit because it is characterized by negative, deficit thinking. Valenzuela (1999) refers to the effect of this deficit thinking as subtractive schooling. Lindsey, Nuri Robins, and Terrell (2010) consider deficit thinking as cultural destructiveness, and they define it as seeking to eliminate the cultures of others in all aspects of the school and in relationship to the community served.

Recently, several hundred principal candidates were asked to identify school-related examples demonstrating the different locations on the cultural highway as they traveled to Cultural Community. The principal candidates gave more examples of Cultural Deficit than any other cultural location. These principal candidates represented school campuses of all sizes and geographic regions—they came from urban, rural, and suburban areas—and the group was characterized by a diversity of ethnicities, religions, languages, sexual orientations, abilities, and socioeconomic statuses. They indicated that much of their time was spent discussing damage to campus climate because of the conflicts surrounding culturally negative experiences. Many of them reported hearing educators make the following painful comments:

- "I just don't understand *those* kids."
- "The school really changed when they created that housing development, and, you will see, those kids are just not teachable."
- "I am sick and tired of those kids speaking Spanish in my class; they just do not want to fit in with us. If they don't want to speak English, they need to go back to where they came from!"
- "Those special ed kids make me uncomfortable. I liked it better when they sent them to their own schools, or at least to those portables or resource rooms."

Unfortunately, because of a lack of understanding or knowledge of cultural issues, faculty members often feel overwhelmed by the different groups on the campus. This often leads to minimizing the needs of these students and maximizing the challenge of how to best support these students. Thus, cultural diversity is often viewed as negative and differences as a deficit.

The following practices are examples of Cultural Deficit thinking that often cause conflict in schools:

- Hiring new teachers who have little or no experience working in diverse educational settings with vast and varied student demographics.
- Blaming low performance ratings for the campus on selected demographic groups (e.g., students with special needs; minority students, especially Hispanic or African American students; economically disadvantaged students; students with limited English proficiency).
- Condemning or discriminating against students who have different religious, socioeconomic, racial, or ethnic backgrounds than the majority of the staff and community surrounding the campus.
- Making derogatory statements or engaging in homophobic jokes, and tolerating behavior that discriminates against students on the basis of their sexual orientation.

- Stereotyping the identity of demographic groups—particularly by making prejudicial comments reflecting feelings that those different from the teachers are inferior or deficient.
- Enforcing or supporting policies and decisions that exclude students and parents who are different than the majority of teachers, or different from those who hold power on the campus.
- Communicating, by actions such as tracking, that little is expected of certain students.
- Failing to provide effective professional development on inclusion for all teachers, not just teachers of special education students.

These practices should cause alarm for all educators working to design, develop, and build cultural communities. Leaders must engage in appropriate strategies to move all stakeholders, including students and parents, beyond the Culture Deficit location on the cultural highway.

**Stop and Consider**

1. What other practices might you see on your campus at Cultural Deficit?
2. Reflect critically on your leadership, and identify situations in which you exhibit Culture Deficit understandings.

The following scenario describes a Cultural Deficit case. As you read it, think of the conflict resolution strategies and skills which would most likely lead to resolution of the conflict described.

## CASE STUDY: ENGLISH-ONLY ON OUR CAMPUS

Selena Gonzales was a new third-grade student at Bowie Elementary School. Selena had been born in a border community in Texas, but her family moved to Mexico when she was one. Her family had recently moved from Mexico, returning to the United States and moving to Middletown ISD. Selena quickly made friends with some other children of Mexican American background. Selena and her friends would sometimes converse in Spanish on the playground and even in some classes when English was not required as part of the classroom activities. Selena and her Spanish-speaking friends were soon confronted by language and ethnic discrimination from some of the staff.

While on playground duty, the Bowie coach told Selena and her friends to speak only English while they were at school. He said he did not want to hear any *foreign talk* at Bowie. A veteran teacher told Selena to do as the coach said. The veteran teacher and the coach agreed that Bowie had sure changed, and they and other teachers were upset because of the low performance of the Limited English Proficient (LEP) students on the state-mandated standardized tests. Selena and her friends felt sad and not wanted. Several of Selena's friends were proficient in English, and they clearly understood everything the coach and veteran teacher had said.

Selena told her bilingual teacher, Ms. Martinez, about the comments of the coach and veteran teacher. Ms. Martinez attempted to talk with the coach, but he held out his extended hand (i.e., "talk to the hand" gesture) and said he didn't want to hear any whining about "those kids." Furthermore, he said he figured "little Ms. Selena and her friends are probably illegals," and suggested that they all needed to go back to Mexico or wherever.

Frustrated, Ms. Martinez complained to the Bowie principal, Mr. Smith, about the coach's remarks. She told Principal Smith that Selena and her friends were very upset. Ms. Martinez also informed Mr. Smith that she frequently speaks with the non-English-speaking parents, and they had also complained about Selena and her friends being targeted and feeling excluded based on some of the comments of the staff.

## Stop and Consider

Review the framework for analyzing cultural conflicts (FACC). Frame the various components of this scenario within that model.

### FRAMING THE SOLUTION WITH THE FACC

Step 1: What is the nature of the conflict? What are examples in the case study that indicate this case is framed within Cultural Deficit?

Step 2: What are the choices (*flight, fight, fix*)? What long-term consequences would be likely to occur if the principal chose *flight*? *Fight*? *Fix*?

Step 3: What strategies should be implemented based on the choices of *flight, fight*, and *fix* and their possible consequences?

Mr. Smith, the principal, decided to fix the conflict and used components of the LIFEline strategies and conflict mediation to encourage the coach, the veteran teacher, and Ms. Martinez to participate in a mediation session. He began by reflecting on what had happened. Through the following process, the principal was able to move the parties to a successful win-win solution, using the strategy of mediation and carefully emphasizing the interpersonal LIFEline strategies.

The principal used the LIFEline skill of empathy. He used role reversal (see appendix 2, number 7) and used "I" instead of "You" statements to express feelings and needs—looking, listening, reconciling, and reframing claims helped to transform the initial conversation. For example, instead of demanding that the coach stop making prejudiced comments to the Hispanic students and threatening that he would be written up, Mr. Smith asked each of them to reframe defensive "You" statements into "I" statements. For example, Ms. Martinez could try to see the issue from the coach's perspective. Thus, she might consider how she would feel if she felt students were saying things behind her back by using a foreign language. (See appendix 3, "I Activity.")

The principal used the LIFEline skills of learning by looking and listening and found a small, comfortable room to promote listening and learning. He seated everyone around the table—no heads of the table—and made sure to have comfortable chairs.

He used appropriate body language—again using skills such as a welcoming smile—and when he was seated, he leaned slightly forward with his forearms resting on the table, made eye contact, and offered smiles and nods as he listened.

He used reflective listening and paraphrasing—after each party expressed his or her perspective and version of events, he made sure he reflected on what had been heard, saying, "So I hear you saying," or "If I understand what you said, you are saying . . ." and then watched for an affirming nod. If corrected about a miscommunication or missed message, the principal said, "Sorry, so you are actually saying . . ." and then waited for an affirmative nod in agreement with his reflective paraphrase. The principal further empowered the parties to contribute to solutions by inviting them to offer "I can . . ." statements instead of "You need to" or "You should" statements.

## Stop and Consider

1. What might be the consequences if the principal had chosen *flight*?
2. What might be the consequences if the principal had chosen *fight*?
3. What other conflict strategies might be implemented to bring this cultural conflict to resolution?

Now go back to the FACC and consider step 4: What might the principal do to help individuals involved in this case and others on the campus also at Cultural Deficit continue on the cultural highway to move closer to Cultural Community?

Clearly this is an example of individuals located at Cultural Deficit. The principal knew that it was important to resolve the conflict between Ms. Martinez, the coach, and the veteran teacher. However, he also reflected that this same deficit attitude existed in others on the campus and in the larger community. He was uncomfortable discussing this issue, but he knew it was necessary to establish a community of learners with the common goal of

Cultural Community. The following are two activities that the principal might implement to begin the cultural conversation with the faculty.

## Activity 1

Research indicates that most become teachers because they want to help young people (Nieto, 2005; Whitaker, 2012). Ask teachers to remember why they became teachers and to share this in small groups. This activity reminds teachers of their own personal expectations to do all that they can to build respectful relationships with students, while at the same time supporting them in academic achievement.

## Activity 2

The principal could engage all faculty members in a conversation about guiding principles and then lead them in writing their own guiding principles for their campus. See the work of F. Campbell Jones, B. Campbell Jones, and Lindsey (2010, p. 19), and the NEA website for teacher code of ethics: www.nea.org/home/30442.htm. A review of your state's code of ethics, focusing specifically on ethical conduct toward students, is also recommended (see Texas Administrative Code, Educators' Code of Ethics, chapter 247: http://info.sos.state.tx.us/pls/pub/readtac$ext.ViewTAC?tac_view=4&ti=19&pt=7&ch=247&rl=Y).

## Stop and Consider

What other suggestions would you make to support the principal in the commitment to continuing on the journey to Cultural Community?

## SUMMARY

This chapter has discussed the location of Cultural Deficit. Cultural Deficit emphasizes oppressive behaviors, low student expectations, exclusion, and tendency to discriminate against others. Individuals of other cultural groups are seen in negative ways. Individuals at Cultural Deficit tend to see those who are different from them as "less than."

## Key Thought

Individuals at Cultural Deficit focus on the negative and find it difficult to value others who are different from them. They tend to see difference as deficit.

## REFLECTION ACTIVITIES

1. When examining your own biases, in relation to what issues do you find yourself at Cultural Deficit?
2. What steps are you taking to move forward on the cultural highway regarding this issue?
3. Describe an example of a Cultural Deficit conflict on your campus.
4. Follow the steps in the FACC to resolve the conflict.

*Chapter Five*

# Second Stop on the Cultural Highway

## *Cultural Denial*

Sometimes, I feel discriminated against, but it does not make me angry. It merely astonishes me. How *can* any deny themselves the pleasure of my company? It's beyond me.

—Zora Neale Hurston

### REMEMBER: CULTURAL DENIAL

Remember the following about Cultural Denial, as discussed in chapter 1:

- Cultural Denial looks like a melting pot, color blindness, equality/sameness, tracking, low expectations, acculturation, and false generosity.
- Cultural Denial says, "Your cultural identity is invisible."
- The practice of Cultural Denial is equal treatment for all, although hidden biases often remain.
- The spotlight is on behavior that is neutral to differences.

Individuals from different cultures move through a process called *acculturation*, which is the process of learning a second culture (Diller & Moule, 2005). This process of becoming part of another culture is visible with changes in diet, dress, and language. The beginning of acculturation is generally observed as individuals begin to reject the minority culture and adopt the cultural norms of the dominant culture.

At Cultural Denial individuals from different cultures not only begin to move away from their cultural practices, but other individuals or groups in the institution into which they are assimilating expect them to become just like everyone else—a common source of conflict. This notion of the melting pot has generally been seen as a positive move and, certainly, it has resulted in individuals and groups becoming "Americanized" more quickly.

Educators at Cultural Denial exhibit color-blind behaviors in how they treat young people, which results in conflict. Many educators work at being color-blind so that they can justify treating all students the same. Some consider this appropriate. However, those farther along on the journey to Cultural Community realize the importance of an individual's cultural identity and how this may affect learning and social interaction. These leaders understand that being color-blind is more negative than it is positive.

Being color-blind conveys to others that their cultural identity is only valuable when it matches the typical or dominant ideal. To extend this Cultural Denial behavior beyond a racial or ethnic perspective, it is possible that some educators think all students learn the same way, all live in three- or four-bedroom homes with a mother and a father, and all choose football and baseball as their favorite sports and apple pie as their favorite dessert. There is little room for differentiated treatment, let alone differentiated instruction, except within narrow parameters that mirror the dominant group. Thus, the cultural identity of a young person who is homeless, prefers Bach to baseball, and speaks a language other than English is often at risk of being ignored.

While there is a surface expectation of equal treatment at Cultural Denial, hidden biases often remain. This happens because the various cultural identities with which students come to school are not considered, rendering these students invisible. Therefore, when a student who is living in poverty, for example, does not do well academically, extra supports that might be needed are often not provided.

Sometimes, using Freire's (1970) concept of "false generosity" at Cultural Denial, educators give excuses for students who have a different cultural identity from that of the dominant culture. These educators don't see children who live in poverty as without value or merit, but instead feel compassion that they are already behind because of their circumstances. They do not fault the student for failing to achieve.

However, since Cultural Denial is a location that emphasizes treating everyone the same, it is not considered within the educator's responsibility to provide these extra supports. In fact, doing so might be considered inappropriate since providing additional supports would not be treating all equally. Instead, it could be seen as giving extra attention or assistance to certain students. One-size solutions seldom fit anyone! Thus, this can become an area of conflict with those faculty members who are farther along the cultural highway on their journey to Cultural Community.

The following comments are representative of the perspective of educators who are at Cultural Denial:

- "I gave him (her) the same information that I gave everyone else. It's not my fault if he (she) still failed."
- "That is how I've always taught, and I'm not going to change now!"
- "I can't treat her differently from everyone else—I have to be fair."
- "I really do feel badly for her, but if I can't extend the test time for everyone, I can't extend it for her either."
- "We must stop making all of these modifications and accommodations for those special education students—it is not fair to our regular students."

All too often, the following practices result in cultural conflict at schools where individuals are located at Cultural Denial:

- A lack of understanding differentiated instruction and how and when to implement it.
- Hiring educators who do not have an understanding of the importance of cultural identity.
- Failing to include training in cultural issues when providing staff development.
- Maintaining low expectations of students from certain cultural backgrounds.
- Failing to emphasize and implement the legal mandates and individualized education plans for students with special needs.
- Tracking students into lower-level courses.
- Teaching students as though they all share the background of the dominant culture.

**Stop and Consider**

1. What other kinds of practices might you see on your campus at Cultural Denial?
2. Reflect critically on your leadership, and identify situations in which you exhibit Cultural Denial understandings.

The following scenario describes a Cultural Denial case. As you read it, think of the conflict resolution strategies and skills which would most likely lead to resolution of the conflict described.

### CASE STUDY: PREJUDICE OR PRINCIPLE

Gary, a sixth-grade student with disabilities at Carver Elementary School, was so excited when his teacher told him that his grades had earned him a place on Carver's Honor Roll. When the Honor Roll was posted, Gary's name was on the list with all of the other Honor Roll students at Carver Junior High.

The next day, when the principal arrived at school, he was met in his office by several teachers and the president of the PTA. They were upset that students like Gary were on the Honor Roll since the work had been modified for them. The principal agreed that these students did receive academic modifications, such as being given more time on tests, having some test questions omitted, and other accommodations.

The principal pointed out that the modifications had been developed at each student's ARD (Admission, Review, and Dismissal) meeting and that they were written in the IEP (Individualized Education Plan). The teachers and the PTA president agreed that students who needed them should receive modifications, but they emphatically said, "Students who receive these special exceptions should not be listed on the Honor Roll with the other students!"

**Stop and Consider**

Review the framework for analyzing cultural conflicts (FACC). Frame the various components of this scenario within that model.

### FRAMEWORK FOR ANALYZING CULTURAL CONFLICTS

> Step 1: What is the nature of the cultural conflict? What examples in the case identify the location of this case as Cultural Denial?
>
> Step 2: What are the choices and the long- and short-term consequences of those choices?
>
> Step 3: What strategies could be implemented based on the choices of *flight*, *fight*, and *fix*, and what are their possible consequences?

Because the purpose of this book is to emphasize strategies for fixing cultural conflict, the principal in this case chooses to fix the conflict. While there are many strategies the principal might use to fix this issue, this case describes the principal's use of invitational theory to resolve the conflict.

The principal reflected on the conflict before him and asked himself if this was really a concern. He knew that if he overlooked this issue, it would only grow into a larger conflict, involving other students and other parents. He also felt that it was wrong to deny recognition to a student who had worked hard and done what was expected as outlined in the student's IEP. Providing a student with appropriate curricular modifications should not be a cause for being excluded from the Honor Roll.

The principal had already conferred with the faculty members privately and explained the policy regarding the Honor Roll and who could be on it at the beginning of the year. In fact, when he had heard rumblings about teacher dissatisfaction regarding this policy a few months ago, he had set up a more formal meeting with the teachers who appeared to be leading this conflict. At that time, he had explained clearly what was expected of the teachers to support this policy.

However, now that the PTA president was also involved, the principal set up a conference with the teachers who had come to his office that morning and included the PTA president. At that meeting, the principal explained his concern and pointed out that he had conferred with the teachers and even held an earlier meeting with them explaining the rationale for the Honor Roll policy regarding students with an IEP.

In this meeting, the principal listened carefully to their reasons why this was "unfair" to the rest of the Honor Roll students. He then framed the conflict using the school's mission statement, which was that "every student had the opportunity to excel to the best of his ability." In this way he was able to frame the conflict from one that was "unfair" to other students to a more individualized approach of what was "fairest" for each individual student.

Next, following the combat aspect of invitational theory, the principal engaged the teachers and the PTA president in discussing a compromise which would be more agreeable to all parties. The principal emphasized that any compromise must not discriminate in excluding students on an IEP from the Honor Roll. The teachers and the PTA president left the meeting feeling that their concerns had been heard, and they scheduled a time to meet together next week, after contacting other educators to see what they were doing, to see if they could find another way to honor all students, including those with an IEP, when grades fell within the Honor Roll range.

## Stop and Consider

1. What are possible consequences if *flight* had been chosen by the principal?
2. What are possible consequences if *fight* had been chosen by the principal?
3. Since the principal chose *fix*, what other strategies might be implemented to bring this cultural conflict to appropriate resolution?

Now go back to the FACC and consider step 4: What might the principal do to help individuals involved in this case and others on the campus also at Cultural Denial or Cultural Deficit continue on to Cultural Community?

The principal recognized the importance of working with teachers and the PTA president at cultural locations of Deficit or Denial. The principal understood the importance of valuing students who have an IEP and also valuing the work they do. The following are suggestions of activities that could move others closer to Cultural Community:

## Activity 1

At a faculty meeting, randomly assign teachers to small groups and invite them to share challenges they have faced while growing up and how they overcame these challenges. This activity builds trust among faculty members and deepens relationships. It also points out that everyone does not have the same challenges, nor are they overcome in the same ways. This emphasizes the need to acknowledge how individuals are different and how needs might change over time.

## Activity 2

Ask faculty members to reflect privately on the following questions:

1. Do you know someone who is gay?
2. Do you have a gay family member?
3. Do you know someone who has been bullied?
4. Do you have a family member who has been bullied?
5. Do you know someone who has lost his or her job recently due to economic cutbacks?
6. Do you have a family member who has lost his or her job recently due to economic cutbacks?
7. Do you know someone who is physically or mentally handicapped?
8. Do you have a family member who is physically or mentally handicapped?
9. Do you know someone who has a learning disability?
10. Do you have a family member who has a learning disability?
11. Do you know someone who is a different ethnicity than you?
12. Do you have a close friend who is a different ethnicity than you?

There are many more questions one can ask. The focus of this activity is to begin to recognize both the different components making up cultural identities and the importance of acknowledging these differences. When the leader feels that a covenant relationship is established, these questions could be discussed in small groups.

## Activity 3

Engage the faculty in a discussion of how the approach of sameness or equality can create problems for individuals. Use the example that to treat everyone equally could mean that no one would be allowed to wear glasses (wear a brace, have extended test time, etc.). How might this affect learning? What can educators do to help students overcome this obstacle?

## Stop and Consider

What other suggestions would you make to support the leader in the commitment to continuing on the journey to Cultural Community?

## SUMMARY

In this chapter, we have considered the location of Cultural Denial, which emphasizes color blindness, lack of recognition of our cultural differences, and the belief that everyone should be treated the same. Individuals who do not acknowledge the cultural identity of others see everyone as "just like me." This results often in failing to provide supports for others that might be needed.

## Key Thought

An individual's cultural identity may affect learning and social interaction. Being color-blind, as we have thought of it previously, is more negative than it is positive. Leaders cannot support others fully if they do not acknowledge cultural identity.

## REFLECTION ACTIVITIES

1. As you critically reflect on your own biases, consider an issue in relation to which you find yourself at Cultural Denial.
2. What steps are you taking to move farther along the cultural highway continuum regarding this issue?
3. Describe an example of a Cultural Denial conflict on your campus.
4. Use the FACC to resolve the conflict to continue on to Cultural Community.

*Chapter Six*

# Next Stop on the Cultural Highway

*Cultural Discovery*

Each of us is a book waiting to be written, and that book, if written, results in a person explained.

—Thomas M. Cirignano, *The Constant Outsider*

## REMEMBER: CULTURAL DISCOVERY

Remember the following about Cultural Discovery from chapter 1:

- Cultural Discovery looks like seeking better understandings, Public Law 94-142 (Education of All Handicapped Children Act, federal law passed in 1975), affirmative action, false generosity, stereotyping, and under-standing the importance of cultural identity
- Cultural Discovery says, "We see you, but we aren't sure what to do."
- The practice of Cultural Discovery is tolerance.
- The spotlight at Cultural Discovery is on accepting differences.

As leaders continue on the cultural highway on their journey to Cultural Community, they reach Cultural Discovery. While awareness of differences among groups is nothing new, at this location the leaders' awareness focuses on a richer understanding or dimension of these differences. Leaders no longer see difference as negative or lacking in value, nor do they ignore the cultural identities associated with differences. Instead, at Cultural Discovery they not only identify that there are differences but tolerate those differences and begin to discover ways to meet these different needs.

Because leaders now see the cultural aspects of those around them in a richer light, they begin to open themselves to building relationships with those who are from different backgrounds. Leaders engage in the discovery process of learning about different cultures. They try new foods and like them. They read about history with broader understandings. Leaders discover that different cultures emphasize learning in different ways, and because of this newfound tolerance for cultural differences, leaders and others are more accepting.

As educational leaders at Cultural Discovery make new discoveries about the kinds of differences that exist among cultures, however, they often fail to know how to accommodate those differences in classrooms and on school campuses, which leads to conflict. Consequently, lesson plans remain much the same, and few changes are made in school policies. When committees are established on the campus, leaders at Cultural Discovery make sure to include *token* individuals of different ethnicities, for example.

When leaders want to conduct a review of student engagement on the campus by ethnicity, for example, they are likely to give this responsibility to someone who is a member of a typically disenfranchised group. When leaders do this, awkward interactions with minority faculty members are created. For example, a leader might go to the one African American female teacher on the faculty and ask her, "Why do all of the African American girls use that ghetto-talk?" Clearly the leader acknowledges the diversity issues with African American students, but at this location on the cultural highway, leaders use responses to these differences that are often inappropriate.

Even though leaders have become more accepting of differences, at Cultural Discovery they still find themselves stereotyping others, which often results in conflict. Leaders do not see the limitations of stereotyping and are not open to the individuality within all groups. In efforts to be tolerant, leaders and other educators continue to fall prey to false generosity and use the circumstances of children as an excuse for having low expectations of success.

The following kinds of conversations are often heard among faculty members and others at Cultural Discovery:

- "I understand that our Native American kids learn best orally, but I just don't have time to incorporate that in my classroom. If I can find time, I'll try to do more oral work with them."
- "I didn't realize that some Asian students and many of their parents were caste conscious. I wonder how to accommodate that cultural difference in the class or in my lesson plans?"
- "No wonder we have so few African American boys in our AP classes; the peer pressure to go into sports is just too much for us to combat. Besides,

many of the African American male students do not want to be labeled as 'school smart'; they prefer the reputation of having 'street smarts.'"

- "I know Kimberly has been an outstanding soccer player for our school, but I still cannot see her being able to compete with our male students in football, and she insists on trying out as a place kicker."

At Cultural Discovery, the following practices on campuses often result in conflict since individuals are at different locations along the cultural highway:

- Committees are established to review student engagement with representation from all student groups but with token members of different ethnicities.
- Faculty members continue to engage in false generosity and tolerate the low achievement of students whose cultural backgrounds are different and often challenging (poverty, for example).
- There is a lack of knowledge regarding how to support the needs of students who learn in a variety of ways.
- The importance of Title IX is acknowledged as opening more opportunities for female students in sports, but gender stereotypes continue to exist.

## Stop and Consider

1.  What other kinds of Cultural Discovery practices do you see on your campus that have the capacity to create conflict?
2.  Reflect critically on your leadership, and identify situations in which you exhibit Cultural Discovery understandings.

Consider the following scenario of a conflict at Cultural Discovery. What conflict resolution strategies would you use to bring about resolution?

### CASE STUDY: HURRICANE HAVOC

Ann Harris was in her second year as superintendent of a low-performing school district of ten thousand students. While the school was still rated as low performing, test scores had actually improved the previous year, so Superintendent Harris was feeling very encouraged at the beginning of this new school year. The school was in a demographically changing area in a coastal region in the southern United States.

Ten years ago, the school population had been 80 percent white, 20 percent black and Hispanic, and 50 percent low socioeconomic status. Today, the school is 55 percent black, 20 percent Hispanic, and 20 percent white, with nearly 5 percent of students from the Middle East; 95 percent of the students are considered economically disadvantaged. What had once been a middle-class neighborhood had changed dramatically to a poor area with run-down housing and numerous low-income apartment buildings.

Soon after the beginning of Superintendent Harris's second year, the district was devastated by a hurricane that created havoc in the area. Thankfully, none of the schools was damaged, and the superintendent and many faculty members worked tirelessly to help students and their families through this difficult time, even driving buses to help people relocate until electricity and water were re-established.

Due to the hurricane, several school days were missed and would have to be made up. After discussing this with district administrators, who had been given suggestions from their staffs, the superintendent recommended to the all-white school board that most of the Saturdays over the next two months would be makeup days. However, they were still in need of one more day. She suggested that this makeup day would be on January 21, which was Martin Luther King Jr. Day. The school board approved the new school calendar.

The next day, as Superintendent Harris entered her office, she noticed that the receptionist appeared frustrated as she answered phone calls. The presidents of each PTA in the district were waiting in the foyer for the superintendent, requesting a special meeting. The meeting lasted less than ten minutes. The PTA presidents told her that parents were furious—how dare the school district hold school on Martin Luther King Jr. Day!

The meeting ended with raised voices. One of the PTA presidents shouted, "Students at our school will NOT be in attendance that day!" Superintendent Harris could not believe that parents were responding this way. Could they not see how hard she and other personnel had worked to help the district after the hurricane? She finally stood up from behind her desk and said quietly, but through clenched teeth, "Any students who do not attend school on Martin Luther King Jr. Day will be considered unexcused and receive zeros for the day and not be allowed to make up the work!" The parents left furious. Superintendent Harris sat down at her desk. She was exhausted. What had she done? Had a whole year's worth of progress just been ruined? She and other administrators had looked at the calendar from dozens of different perspectives, and there had been no other solution.

## Stop and Consider

Review the framework for analyzing cultural conflicts (FACC). Frame the various components of this scenario within that model.

## FRAMING THE CULTURAL CONFLICT WITH THE FACC

Step 1: What is the nature of the conflict? What are the issues in this case that suggest that the leader was at Cultural Discovery?

Step 2: Superintendent Harris has three choices: *flight, fight,* and *fix.* What might the consequences be of each choice?

Step 3: What strategies should be implemented based on the choices of *flight, fight,* and *fix* and their possible consequences?

Reviewing the five styles of conflict management based on the work of Thomas (1976), the superintendent recognized that this was an issue that needed to be handled immediately. Therefore, avoidance was not a strategy to be considered. She also realized that compromise was not possible at this point since the calendar had been considered by school personnel, and the district must comply with state attendance guidelines. Superintendent Harris acknowledged that failing to involve parents and community leaders in the decision had exacerbated the problem; thus, being assertive without their cooperation had actually contributed to an escalation of this conflict.

The superintendent considered the style of accommodation but realized that in this situation, it was not possible to accommodate the parent demands regarding this attendance date this year. She knew that in this case, a collaborative response would be most effective. Therefore, she invited parents and community leaders to a meeting to discuss the situation. Because there were no available dates left in the school calendar for this year, she conceded that there would be no negative consequences for students who did not attend school on Martin Luther King Jr. Day.

In a win-win solution for all, a committee was formed to look at next year's calendar and build in possible dates for unexpected events such as hurricanes. By being open to listening and working with parents and others to find a balanced resolution for this year and future years, this decision was both high in assertiveness and in cooperation.

### Stop and Consider

1. What short- and long-term consequences might occur if the superintendent had chosen *flight*?
2. If the superintendent chose to *fight*, what short- and long-term consequences might occur?
3. What other conflict resolution strategies might the leader use to resolve this conflict?

Now go back to the FACC and consider step 4: What might the leader do to help individuals involved in this case, and others within her community—

including faculty who are at Cultural Discovery or earlier stages of their cultural journey—to do in the commitment to continue on to Cultural Community?

The superintendent recognized that many in her district were struggling with understanding Cultural Discovery and earlier locations on the journey. While individuals in the district were moving forward to better understand the diverse population of students, there was still a need to demonstrate that they valued and appreciated the varied aspects of culture. Following are suggestions to bring individuals in the district farther along on the cultural highway and closer to Cultural Community.

## Activity 1

Ask individuals on your campus who have different traditions at Christmas or other holidays to share what they do and why. This allows participants to understand that all have cultural influences and experiences within their families that might differ from their own.

## Activity 2

Create a task force of educators and parents to review ways to focus on forming parent-school partnerships with a diverse group of parents. This increases dialogue and builds relationships among stakeholders (Hutchins, Greenfeld, Epstein, Sanders, & Galindo, 2012).

## Activity 3

Because Cultural Discovery is often rooted in stereotyping conditions, a professional development activity that involves the faculty and encourages discussion would be valuable. One example of such an activity is called "The Effect of Stereotypes: What's in a Label?" (Goldstein, 1997). The goal of the activity is to demonstrate how stereotypes affect the self-perception and behavior of the person who is stereotyped. Here are the directions:

- Using adhesive labels, write a stereotypic attribute on each label. Some examples include *violent, athletic, cute, overemotional, incompetent, good at math, lazy, untrustworthy, unclean, musical, materialistic, diseased, unintelligent, exotic, forgetful,* and *frail.*
- Discuss stereotyping, and explain that you will conduct a simulation exercise to help faculty consider how stereotypes work. Next, attach a label on each faculty member's forehead (or back), so that the label is not visible to the wearer. Make clear that these labels are being assigned randomly and have nothing to do with anyone's actual attributes. (You may want to assign some faculty members the role of observers.)

- Now ask faculty members to spend five to ten minutes talking with each other about academic goals for the year. Tell faculty they should circulate in order to talk with several different people and that they should *treat one another according to the other person's labeled attribute*. For example, someone labeled "forgetful" might be repeatedly reminded of the instructions.
- After five to ten minutes, reconvene, but leave the labels on for a little while longer. Ask faculty to share how they felt during the exercise, how they were treated by others, and how this treatment affected them. Faculty members are likely to mention their discomfort not only with being stereotyped but with treating others stereotypically. Then remove the labels.
- Then discuss how stereotyping might have an influence on how students are treated and also on how students respond.

## SUMMARY

In this chapter we have considered the location of Cultural Discovery, which emphasizes seeking better understandings of cultural issues, and explored how our understanding of cultural issues affects learning and how we interact with others. Individuals at Cultural Discovery see cultural differences but often do not know how to accommodate for them appropriately.

### Key Thought

Leaders discover that different cultures emphasize learning in different ways, and because of this new-found tolerance for cultural differences, leaders and others are more accepting.

## REFLECTION ACTIVITIES

1. As you critically reflect, in relation to what cultural issues do you find yourself at Cultural Discovery?
2. What steps are you taking to move forward to Cultural Community?
3. Describe an example of a Cultural Discovery conflict on your campus or in your district.
4. What would you do to resolve the conflict and continue on to Cultural Community?

*Chapter Seven*

# Next Stop on the Cultural Highway

## *Cultural Celebration*

What we have to do . . . is to find a way to celebrate our diversity and debate our differences without fracturing our communities.

—Hillary Clinton

### REMEMBER: CULTURAL CELEBRATION

Before reading the chapter, review the information about Cultural Celebration, which is discussed in chapter 1.

- Cultural Celebration looks like a salad bowl, a discussion which acknowledges prejudice, celebrating events such as Cinco de Mayo, seeking common ground, identifying achievement gaps, and moving toward integration.
- Cultural Celebration says, "You are invited to come in."
- The practice at Cultural Celebration emphasizes acknowledgment of other cultures.
- The spotlight is on the appreciation and increased value of diversity.

As leaders move farther along the cultural highway, conflicts continue to occur because others on the school campus are at many different locations on this journey. When individuals are at the highway marker of Cultural Celebration, they recognize the importance of the acculturation process and view cultural integration as an important step forward.

At Cultural Celebration, leaders and others have reached a location that acknowledges the value of diversity and also recognizes the importance of celebrating and including diverse cultural events within the school curriculum, which in itself can be a source of conflict. Teaching units have been developed to emphasize special times during the school year, such as Martin Luther King Jr. Day, Black History Month, and Cinco de Mayo. At Thanksgiving, many educators emphasize the study of Native Americans. During the holiday season, there is an emphasis on how students around the world celebrate.

Administrators and teachers spend time reviewing data and considering specifically how various groups respond on standardized test results to identify where achievement gaps might occur. They focus on the achievement gap not to place blame, but to begin to accommodate the needs of diverse groups of children.

At Cultural Celebration, the focus moves from noticing how different individuals are to seeking common ground. Instead of emphasizing differences, now individuals consider in what ways groups are alike. Thus, at Cultural Celebration, practice acknowledges other cultures in a way that values diversity. Having traveled away from the melting pot at previous locations, leaders are now fully appreciative of the salad bowl effect and acknowledge how the diversity brings a richer experience to their personal and professional lives.

At Cultural Celebration, individuals acknowledge during conversations and discussions that all have prejudices and biases, but this leads to conflict, because these behaviors are most likely to be seen in others rather than in themselves. The very isolation of school events, such as Black History Month, within the curriculum can be a source of conflict.

In other words, Celebration is a positive location where special diversity days are built into the curriculum. Conflicts arise, however, when others are not this far along on the cultural highway and disagree, or when attempts are made to move beyond the "calendar" and integrate positive acknowledgments of different cultural groups throughout the curriculum. There is often the notion that this should be the end of the cultural journey and that there is no need for further travel.

Another cause of conflict at Cultural Celebration is the sense that one is doing all that can and should be done. For example, while it has been identified that there is an achievement gap among groups of students, individuals have not yet fully committed to doing all that needs to be done to provide support for students to bridge the academic achievement gap. Too often, leaders and other school constituents feel that since they are not able to change the circumstances of poverty or parental noninvolvement, for example, it is enough to celebrate special days of differing cultures.

Individuals at Cultural Celebration engage in reflective discussions, and often they are able to openly and candidly acknowledge prejudices and biases toward groups different from them. However, comments indicative of cultural conflict might include the following:

- "I try, but I just don't understand why these young kids [parents, teachers] do . . ."
- "I'm not comfortable working with people who are gay; I admit it. That's just how I am."
- "I understand that those apartment kids have some challenges, and I'll help when I can, but I'm not going out of my way . . . after all, there's just so much time in the day."
- "I see that our Hispanic [black, Indian, etc.] kids have lower math scores. Their parents just aren't willing to help."
- "That's not how we did it in MY day!"

Common practices that occur on school campuses reflecting the location of Cultural Celebration, and that often result in conflict, include the following:

- Limiting celebrations to specific calendar days—Black History Month, Cinco de Mayo, etc.
- Inserting books or stories by ethnically diverse writers into the curriculum to make sure that there is at least one black writer, one Hispanic writer, perhaps one writer from the Middle East . . . but no more.
- Identifying where prejudices or biases exist in others, but not engaging in critical reflection on ourselves.
- Moving toward integration in such a way that it is enough that campus groups have at least one or two representatives from each group, but such representation sometimes is seen as appointing a token minority to the group.
- Using test data to identify where achievement gaps exist, then providing only limited support to bridge that gap.

**Stop and Consider**

1. What other kinds of practices might you see on your campus at Cultural Celebration?
2. Reflect critically on your leadership, and identify situations in which you exhibit Cultural Celebration understandings.

The following scenario describes a case at the location of Cultural Celebration. As you read it, think of the conflict resolution strategies and skills which would most likely lead to resolution of the conflict described.

## CASE STUDY: WE GAVE YOU A
## WHOLE MONTH FOR CELEBRATION

Jennifer Joy, a third-year high school math teacher and new cheerleader sponsor, was very excited that the varsity football team had made it to the quarterfinals in the playoffs. She knew Mr. Olde, a career assistant principal, was planning on a special pep rally to send the football team and cheerleaders off to the playoff game.

Mr. Olde often asked Ms. Joy to do some special cheers for the students. Ms. Joy visited with Mr. Olde on Monday prior to the Friday pep rally. Ms. Joy was proud of the diversity among the cheerleaders, since the squad included white, African American, and Hispanic students. Ms. Joy informed Mr. Olde that the cheerleaders had worked on a terrific rap that would energize the students, staff, and community members attending the pep rally. She said the rap incorporated some of the better lyrics from contemporary hip-hop artists, and she even shared the lyrics with Mr. Olde.

Mr. Olde had a puzzled look on his face and said, "Ms. Joy, those kids have a whole month to celebrate their heritage—we have Black History Month. Maybe you can help them develop a rap for their Black History program." She told Mr. Olde that she and other math teachers had been using rap to teach math functions and concepts throughout the year. He was not persuaded; in fact, he wondered aloud if it was a good idea to bring this "stuff" into the curriculum at all. He then suggested that she return to some of the more traditional cheers—"Save that rap stuff for their month."

Ms. Joy left the meeting in tears and went straight to the principal's office to discuss this issue with him. His secretary set up a meeting for first thing the next morning, when he could address the conflict with both Ms. Joy and Mr. Olde in attendance.

### Stop and Consider

Review the framework for analyzing cultural conflicts (FACC). Frame the various components of this scenario within that model.

## FRAMING THE CULTURAL CONFLICT WITH THE FACC

Step 1: What is the nature of the conflict? What details in the case suggest that the conflict is located at Cultural Celebration?

Step 2: What are the choices? What are the consequences of those choices?

Step 3: What strategies should be implemented based on the choices of *flight, fight,* and *fix* and their possible consequences?

The principal chose *fix*: he decided that he would follow the principles of mediation and that he would be the mediator. Here are the resolution strategies that he followed:

The principal began by explaining the purpose of this mediation conversation. After Mr. Olde and Ms. Joy seated themselves at the round table in his office, he commented that the purpose of this meeting was not to judge right or wrong, but instead, to listen to one another to resolve this conflict.

The principal asked both individuals to acknowledge agreement by saying "Yes" to the following ground rules:

- Remaining seated.
- Not interrupting.
- Being honest.
- Not condemning either person's role in the disagreement.
- Keeping the conversation in the office confidential among the three of them.
- Agreeing to solve the problem.

The principal began by inviting Ms. Joy to talk about what prompted her to come to his office in tears yesterday. He asked Mr. Olde to listen carefully, and if he had questions about the situation, to ask those questions after she had finished talking. He emphasized that it was imperative that Mr. Olde understand the conflict from Ms. Joy's perspective, as well as to acknowledge her feelings, which caused her to cry in frustration.

After Ms. Joy finished discussing the issue and Mr. Olde had asked his questions to better understand, Mr. Olde was given the same opportunity to discuss the conflict. Ms. Joy was provided time to ask clarifying questions for her own understanding. Several times during each person's discussion, the principal clarified statements by commenting, "I hear you saying . . ."

Then each individual was asked to assume the role of the other and discuss how they might feel if they were the other person. For example, the principal said to Mr. Olde, "If you were Ms. Joy and had been asked to put together a special cheer for the pep rally, how would you feel?" Then he said to Ms. Joy, "Knowing that Mr. Olde is in charge of approving the pep rally activities, how would you feel?"

The principal then emphasized the importance of working together as a faculty and asked each to brainstorm ways they could resolve the conflict. In other words, he asked Ms. Joy how she could contribute to a resolution of the conflict, and then he asked Mr. Olde what suggestions he could make that would resolve the conflict.

After both discussed the conflict in this manner, Mr. Olde acknowledged his appreciation that Ms. Joy had openly shared the cheer they had created. He also expressed his appreciation that she was willing to follow through with this responsibility. He even admitted that the pep rally was "for the kids," so doing a rap "probably made sense." At the same time, Ms. Joy acknowledged how much she appreciated Mr. Olde's support in scheduling this special pep rally for the students. She agreed that they would also include some of the more traditional cheers.

## Stop and Consider

1. What might the consequences be if the leader chose *flight*?
2. What might the consequences be if the leader chose *fight*?
3. What other strategies might be implemented to resolve this conflict?

Now go back to the FACC and consider step 4: What might the principal do to help individuals involved in the case, and others also at Cultural Celebration or other locations on the Cultural Community journey, to continue on to Cultural Community?

Cultural Celebration is a location that has recognized in a positive way the differences rooted in cultural issues. However, in this case, it is apparent that the differences in age create a conflict in understanding between the assistant principal and the cheerleader sponsor. Because the principal wants to improve understandings of Cultural Celebration, the following are suggested activities for the leader committed to continuing on to Cultural Community.

## Activity 1

Invite a parent or educator to share their story about any of the twelve cultural markers mentioned in chapter 1. Remember that these cultural attributes include race, ethnicity/nationality, social class, sex/gender, health, age, geographic region, sexuality, religion, social status, language, and ability/disability. Encourage them to discuss how this aspect of culture affected their learning and participation in school events.

## Activity 2

Assign faculty to work as partners. Make assignments of partnerships based on a mix of the twelve cultural markers. The assignment is for partners to brainstorm a list of things they have in common. After fifteen minutes, the partners report back to the group to talk about what they learned. The purpose of the activity is to build bridges of understanding between individuals who appear to be different from us. Engaging in dialogue about what we have in common increases our value and respect for others. See Withers and Lewis (2003, pp. 33–35) for a complete discussion of this activity.

**Activity 3**

Ask faculty members to privately reflect on identifying biases they might have that are changing as they learn more about cultural influences. Provide time to do this in a faculty meeting or at a retreat.

**Stop and Consider**

1. What is an example of a Cultural Celebration conflict that has occurred at your campus in which you were involved?
2. What other suggestions would you make to support the leader in the commitment to continuing on the journey to Cultural Community?

## SUMMARY

This chapter has considered the location of Cultural Celebration. Cultural Celebration emphasizes the value of others and their cultural experiences and identities. Individuals at Cultural Celebration acknowledge the achievement gap and work toward reducing that gap.

**Key Thought**

At Cultural Celebration the focus moves from noticing how different others are to seeking common ground.

## REFLECTION ACTIVITIES

1. As you critically reflect on your own growth, in relation to what issues do you find yourself at Cultural Celebration?
2. What steps are you taking to move forward to Cultural Community?
3. Describe an example of a Cultural Celebration conflict on your campus or in your district.
4. What strategies would you implement to resolve that conflict?

*Chapter Eight*

# Next Stop on the Cultural Highway

## Cultural Conscience

> The challenge of social justice is to evoke a sense of community that we need to make our nation a better place, just as we make it a safer place.
> —Marian Wright Edelman

### REMEMBER: CULTURAL CONSCIENCE

Before reading the chapter, review information about Cultural Conscience, which is discussed in chapter 1.

- Cultural Conscience looks like appreciation of diversity, difficult conversations which examine one's own biases as well as institutional biases, integration, accommodation, bridging the achievement gap, and equity.
- Cultural Conscience says, "Let's join together."
- The practice of Cultural Conscience is cooperation.
- The spotlight is on social justice.

As the cultural highway is traveled, at Cultural Conscience, the journey's goal of Cultural Community is getting near. At Cultural Conscience, leaders have a full appreciation of other cultures and acknowledge the rich diversity this brings to the school campus. Diversity is considered a strength that contributes to a positive campus climate.

The importance of establishing covenant relationships within the school community was noted in chapter 2. Sergiovanni (1996) emphasizes that covenant relationships are developed by (1) respecting and valuing diversity, (2) nurturing shared values and beliefs through commitment to a shared vision,

(3) serving the common good by endeavoring to promote unity, and (4) supporting people as they help one another achieve common purposes.

At Cultural Conscience, leaders build on the covenant relationship by engaging in critical conversations about culture and the resultant conflicts. While these conversations are still difficult, leaders are more comfortable because of the trust level that has been achieved on the campus between all stakeholders. Leaders are critically reflective and recognize and examine their own biases. They no longer acknowledge biases with the excuse, "Well, that's just how I am." Instead, leaders reflect on what can be done to overcome and work through the limitations of their biases as they engage with others who have different backgrounds and experiences from their own.

On the school campus, leaders focus on understanding the distinction between equity and equality. In this way, they are no longer as concerned about everyone having equal opportunity as they are concerned to do what they can to provide equitable opportunities, such as implementing support mechanisms of tutoring, mentoring, or differentiated instruction, for example.

At Cultural Conscience, leaders work cooperatively and collaboratively with teachers, athletic coaches, and parents to support students. They conduct equity audits (see appendix 4) to review student standardized testing scores and student involvement as they seek to identify the learning gaps or involvement gaps, then share this information and strategize ways to bridge the gaps (Harris & Hopson, 2008; Skrla, McKenzie, & Scheurich, 2009). Leaders also conduct equity audits to consider institutional practices, such as diversity of school activity participation. They talk about the notion of social justice, which Franklin D. Roosevelt defined as "the path of faith, the path of hope, and the path of love toward our fellow man" (FDR Quotes, www.goodreads.com/quotes).

At Cultural Conscience, comments such as these can result in conflict when leaders consider that individuals and groups on the campus are at different locations on the cultural highway:

- "We can't change our students' home lives, but we can better meet their needs at school."
- "It's not enough to celebrate Black History Month [Cinco de Mayo, etc.]; we need to celebrate these students every day."
- "These kids who come from poverty have all kinds of challenging experiences. What can we do at school to support their needs?"
- "We cannot restore their sight [hearing], but we can provide the necessary tools that will enable students who are visually [hearing] impaired to succeed to the best of their ability."
- "We need to make the body of literature in our reading programs more diverse, even though our school population is not diverse."

What practices are most common in our schools when leadership is located at Cultural Conscience?

- Educators conduct equity audits and share findings with all stakeholders, including school board members, parents, and other stakeholders.
- Educators emphasize ethnic diversity; for example, through literature and bringing in diverse speakers, regardless of the homogeneous nature of the school population.
- Educators cooperate with community organizations to provide for students' needs, including implementing full-service schools with health clinics and nutrition centers.
- Educational leaders implement professional development that includes focused, culturally appropriate teaching strategies, and learning accommodations and modifications for students with special needs.

## Stop and Consider

1. What other practices might you see on your campus at Cultural Conscience?
2. Reflect critically on your leadership, and identify situations in which you exhibit Cultural Conscience understandings.

The following scenario is an example of a conflict at Cultural Conscience. As you read it, think of the conflict resolution strategies and skills which would most likely lead to resolution of the conflict described.

### CASE STUDY: DISAGGREGATING THE DATA— THAT'S JUST TOO MUCH!

As Principal Ann Jones reviewed the latest set of demographic information for her middle school campus located in a large city in the south, she reflected on how the student population continued to change, just as had been predicted. Only a few years ago, the school had been populated with mostly white, middle- to low-income families. Now the student population had grown to be 51 percent Hispanic, 15 percent black, 5 percent Asian, a growing population of students from the Middle East, and about 25 percent white. Nearly 90 percent of the students were classified as low socioeconomic status, and this number would continue to climb since nearby industries were closing.

In contrast, while reviewing the files on the returning teachers, Principal Jones noticed that the teaching staff had experienced very few changes over the past ten years. Over 80 percent of the returning teachers were white women, and most were over forty and had been at the middle school for over ten years. She observed that none of the teachers lived in the school attendance zone. One teacher had recently told her, "This used to be a great neighborhood. I know, because I grew up here, but it has changed so much, I wouldn't think of living here now."

The district, which was now a low-income, urban district with mostly minority students, continued to recruit new teachers from colleges in states up north, such as Minnesota. In fact, the few young teachers were nearly all from those northern states; they came eager to teach and were idealistic, of course, but most of them came to enjoy the warm weather in the south, she thought.

The district had implemented many curriculum changes, such as reading more multicultural stories at each grade level. Speakers of varying ethnicities were invited to the campus to share their stories. Cultural celebrations were held nearly each month to recognize different groups. However, student scores on the standardized achievement tests were still low. At the first in-service meeting of the year, Ms. Jones had handed out copies of the math and reading scores and invited the teachers to consider the scores by different groups of students and highlight where gaps were visible.

After the in-service meeting, two of her most trusted teachers came to her with disturbing news. Many of the older teachers were complaining loudly about being expected to do too much. Now they were expected to disaggregate the achievement scores. This was entirely too much! The conflict was not just with these older teachers. Some of the newer teachers were overheard in the faculty lounge complaining that they were afraid that since the scores were so low, now they would have to give up their Saturdays to tutor or mentor or provide other individualized interventions. To make matters worse, many of the new teachers worried that they would be labeled poor teachers since they were at a low-performing campus!

## Stop and Consider

Review the framework for analyzing cultural conflicts (FACC). Frame the various components of this scenario within that model.

### FRAMING THE SOLUTION WITH THE FACC

Step 1: What is the nature of the conflict? Cultural Conscience and conflict issues seem to be rooted in geographic location, ageism, and poverty.

Step 2: What are the choices? What are the consequences of those choices?

Step 3: What conflict strategies should be implemented based on the principal's decision to fix the conflict?

Ms. Jones decided to analyze the conflict and conflict management strategies using some of the knowledge and skills she had learned during a session on "Conflict Resolution for School Leaders" at a state administrators' conference. The session reviewed the common strategies used in corporate training and, more recently, as applied to school settings. These tools included negotiation, mediation, and arbitration.

Ms. Jones had used the mediation strategies to resolve many of one-on-one personnel issues and, in some cases, parent and teacher conflicts, and had even trained a campus peer-mediation team of students that had been very successful in reducing many of the day-to-day conflicts among students. But this case appeared too large to be resolved through mediation.

Arbitration, with Ms. Jones being the arbitrator, might result in compliance with her directives, but she did not feel it would result in teachers and support staff being truly invested in disaggregating data to implement individualized instructional plans to ensure that all students succeed in academic improvement. So she decided to utilize one of the negotiation strategies she was taught at the session.

Ms. Jones used the scheduled half-day for teacher workshops to meet with all the teachers together in the school's all-purpose room. Custodians set up round tables and placed five or six chairs around each table. Each table had a sign indicating a number, such as Team 1, Team 2, Team 3, etc. She gave each team a set of guidelines to facilitate the negotiation and conversations. Each team had at least one member of the campus site-based decision-making committee.

The guidelines emphasized giving each participant a voice, and some of the key strategies included were:

- Reflective listening—Each teacher expressed his or her perspective on the disaggregating data duty now being asked of the teachers; before the next teacher stated his or her view, he or she paraphrased what the previous speaker had said (e.g., "So, Ms. Smith, I am hearing you say . . . ," "Mr. Jackson, your concern seems to be . . ."). This was greeted with affirmative nodding and, in some cases, smiling from the previous speaker, because the speaker had been affirmed and validated—"Finally, someone at least understands my point of view."
- Role reversal and engaged empathy—Each teacher or support staff member was asked to assume the role of parent, student, or principal and discuss the achievement challenges from each of those roles, including answering the question, "If you were the parent of this student, how would you *feel* if your son or daughter continued to have low academic achieve-

ment?" All teachers seemed to better understand how the students, parents, and principal felt about this problem. This helped them "walk in the other person's shoes" and identify the feelings involved, which engaged the participant's empathy.

- Solutions, not excuses—At this stage, each participant was asked to brainstorm at least one solution to this problem without judgment or interruption. Each team had to discuss the short- and long-term consequences of each proposed solution. The exercise was not timed, but each team had to reach consensus on their best five or six resolutions. These mutually agreed solutions were reported to the whole group without comment until all solutions were presented.

Ms. Jones was pleased with these resolution activities because the solutions recommended affirmed the goals of the mission, which were to disaggregate data, to design implementation strategies, and to improve achievement for all students.

## Stop and Consider

1. What might the consequences be if the principal chose *flight*?
2. What might the consequences be if the principal chose *fight*?
3. What other strategies might be implemented to bring this cultural conflict to resolution?

Now go back to the FACC and consider step 4: What might the principal do to help individuals involved in this Cultural Conscience case and others on the campus at various stages of the cultural journey continue on to Cultural Community?

The campus principal recognized that her faculty consisted of individuals who were at many locations on the road to Cultural Community. She understood the importance of emphasizing Cultural Conscience in order to continue on the journey to Cultural Community. The following activities are suggested to help in this process.

## Activity 1

Engage the faculty in collaboratively conducting an equity audit to identify academic achievement gaps (see appendix 4).

## Activity 2

Engage the faculty in collaboratively conducting an equity audit to identify institutional practices that appear biased on the campus or within the district (see appendix 4).

## Activity 3

Share stories in faculty meetings of student challenges and their successes. Discuss the strategies that were employed to bring about these successes.

## SUMMARY

This chapter has considered the location of Cultural Conscience. Cultural Conscience emphasizes an appreciation of diversity and has a focus on equity. At Cultural Conscience, educators work toward attaining cooperation and collaboration with all stakeholders.

## Key Thought

At Cultural Conscience, leaders are concerned about doing what they can to provide equitable opportunities, such as implementing support mechanisms like tutoring, mentoring, or differentiated instruction.

## REFLECTION ACTIVITIES

1. When critically reflecting personally, in relation to what issues do you find yourself at Cultural Conscience?
2. What steps are you taking to move forward to Cultural Community?
3. Describe an example of a Cultural Conscience conflict on your campus.
4. What would you do to resolve the conflict and continue on to Cultural Community?

*Chapter Nine*

# Cultural Community

In every community, there is work to be done. In every nation, there are wounds to heal. In every heart, there is the power to do it.
—Marianne Williamson

## REMEMBER: CULTURAL COMMUNITY

Review the information in chapter 1 about Cultural Community:

- Cultural Community looks like discourse which affirms individuals, critical reflection, identifying and meeting needs for all, high standards for all, building positive relationships with others, positive acculturation, integration, and transformational leadership.
- Cultural Community says, "We all belong."
- The practice of Cultural Community is collaboration.
- The floodlight is on the entire landscape.

At Cultural Community, leaders are able to move beyond the focus on cultural differences and cultural likenesses. Now leaders focus on a basic respect for our shared humanity. Having identified and acknowledged the previous locations, leaders know that they can move forward to work with everyone as part of a community of learners and not as separate cultural entities.

While one would like to think that once Cultural Community is reached, all conflict ceases, this is of course unrealistic. Even if everyone agreed on the tenets of Cultural Community and leaders firmly established a covenant of understanding, our very individuality ensures that there will still be conflict. Then, too, clearly not everyone on the campus and within the community will be at the same location on the cultural journey. Some individuals will still be at Deficit, Denial, Discovery, Celebration, or Conscience in relation to different issues of culture.

In fact, leaders will also find that they are at different locations on the cultural highway regarding different issues. For example, a leader may have reached Cultural Community when dealing with ethnic or racial issues, but be at Cultural Discovery when faced with issues of sexuality or ageism.

Leaders who have arrived at Cultural Community must still be adept and knowledgeable regarding conflict strategies. There will continue to be conflicts about the best strategies for identifying and meeting the needs of all students. Occasionally, these conflicts arise when educators do not know how to construct learning activities that address all learners; other times they arise because of persistent biases and prejudices.

Sometimes it is difficult for educators to understand that maintaining high standards for all students means that the standards may need to differ based on students needs, abilities, and experiences. Instead of the mantra being "all children can learn," leaders should be saying "all children can learn, but at different speeds and in different ways." The job of leaders is to encourage educators to identify that learning style and that high standard for individual children.

Positive acculturation at Cultural Community indicates that all individuals have the opportunity to be integrated into classroom, campus, and district activities without regard to cultural markers such as race, ethnicity, or gender. Positive relationships with others transcend cultural barriers also. When individuals reflect on friendships and associations with others, issues of sexual identity, race, age, or ability, for example, are no longer at the forefront. However, because the dialogue and discourse at Cultural Community are open and courageous, there are times when individuals get their feelings hurt or misunderstand another's intent.

Conflict still occurs. An example of conflict at Cultural Community occurred recently at an elementary school due to awards given at the end-of-year awards assembly. The leadership at this school had been working diligently to encourage ethnic minority students. Consequently, some awards were given specifically for Hispanic and black students for their good behavior. However, this resulted in conflict because many parents felt it was inappropriate to give any award based on ethnicity.

Another recent conflict occurred when a popular and excellent male teacher was seen holding hands with another man. Upon hearing this, the superintendent directed the principal to terminate the teacher. The principal, however, stood up for the teacher and decided he would try to resolve the issue in favor of the teacher, despite knowing that this might affect his own job security. A situation such as this can occur in any community because it is unlikely that all stakeholders will reach Cultural Community at the same time regarding the many issues that make up cultural identity.

At Cultural Community, comments such as these can result in conflict, because individuals and groups on the campus are at different locations on the cultural highway:

- "In reviewing the history texts, I don't see a balanced representation of Arabic contributions."
- "Our students of poverty have resilience and strength. What are we doing to utilize those strengths during the school day?"
- "As a teacher, I need to build positive relationships with my students so that they know I support them, even though I am insisting that their work improve."
- "Our faculty has a wide diversity of ages and experience, but we are collaborating on ways to integrate technology into the curriculum, and it's working!"

What practices that occur at Cultural Community are most likely to result in conflict when others are not yet at the same destination?

- After educators conduct equity audits and share findings with all stake-holders, creating collaborative teams to adjust learning activities.
- Implementing professional development that includes differentiated in-struction as needed.
- Collaborating with community organizations to provide for students' needs, including implementing full-service schools with health clinics and nutrition centers.
- Engaging faculty in candid discourse that addresses biases and prejudices.

**Stop and Consider**

1. What other kinds of practices might you see on your campus at Cultu-ral Community?
2. Reflect critically on your leadership, and identify situations in which you exhibit Cultural Community understandings

The following scenario is an example of a conflict at Cultural Community. As you read it, think of the conflict resolution strategies and skills which would most likely lead to resolution of the conflict described.

CASE STUDY: THE DIGITAL DIVIDE

The superintendent of a rural school had spent the past five years working diligently to bring the individuals in his school district to a better understanding of cultural issues. When he became superintendent, the student body was 70 percent black, 15 percent Hispanic, 15 percent white and 90 percent low income. The administrative and teaching staff was 100 percent white.

The superintendent had gone to specialized educator associations, such as the Association of African American Administrators and the Hispanic Administrators Association, to recruit highly qualified administrators and teachers so that the administrative and teaching staff would better match the diversity of the student population. The faculty was now more ethnically diverse, with 25 percent of the faculty either black or Hispanic. The superintendent provided professional development that emphasized cultural proficiency, including training in ESL strategies and implementing comprehensive inclusion.

The faculty conducted equity audits of academic achievement test scores and also conducted an institutional equity audit to ensure that all students were engaged in campus activities. The district academic achievement gap was shrinking noticeably.

At a school board meeting last year, the decision had been made to emphasize technology throughout the district—a decision which the superintendent and other administrators supported. However, there was a sharp divide among the teaching faculty. Younger teachers applauded the decision of the school board; however, many of the teachers over forty were unhappy about the move. In an effort to please both younger and older faculty, the district allocated a considerable amount of money to upgrading technology throughout the district, including new computers for classrooms.

However, the superintendent was becoming aware that older teachers in the district were not making use of the new technology. In fact, the rumor mill was busy. The superintendent heard that they had decided that they were simply going to teach as they always had. They insisted that most of their students had no access to computers anyway, due to poverty and lack of parental support. These teachers also insisted that incomplete assignments that required computers only added to the problem.

The superintendent sat at his desk. He was discouraged. He had tried so hard to help students, educators, and community stakeholders to be more accepting of one another. Yet this conflict was growing. Teachers in the district were actually taking sides: those for technology and those against. What could he do now to resolve this conflict?

## Stop and Consider

Review the framework for analyzing cultural conflicts (FACC). Frame the various components of this scenario within that model.

## FRAMING THE SOLUTION WITH THE FACC

Step 1: What are the cultural natures of the conflict? The conflict seems to be based on issues of ageism and poverty, and individuals are at a variety of different locations on their cultural journeys.

Step 2: What are the choices and their consequences?

Step 3: What conflict strategies did the superintendent implement?

The superintendent chose *fix*. He then implemented the following strategies in resolving the conflict.

The superintendent recognized the importance of using a collaborative style, which is one of the five styles of conflict management. He wanted this to be a win-win solution for all. He valued cooperation *with* all of the faculty and *among* all faculty members, yet he was assertive in emphasizing the need to resolve the conflict.

He understood that it was important for him to communicate wisely and use positive interpersonal skills; therefore, he utilized several LIFEline strategies. He began with being completely involved. At the beginning of the professional development session, he shared the conflict openly with every-one—both the conflict regarding technology and that regarding poverty. He then challenged all to be creative in a brainstorming session.

Because this conflict appeared to be one of ageism or generational differences, he learned by looking and listening. He spent time learning about generational differences himself. He then used professional development days to place faculty members together, being sure that multiple age levels were represented. He then engaged the small groups in reflective listening activities, which utilized paraphrasing or summarizing, with technology as the focus. He also shared specific information regarding poverty issues and challenged faculty members to reflect on ways that they could bridge this gap.

The next LIFEline the superintendent implemented was that of being empathetic. As an administrator who was past forty years of age, he was able to empathize with and affirm the feelings of those older educators who were resistant to the technology change. Acknowledging some of his personal technology concerns publicly opened the opportunity for dialogue between older and younger faculty members. He was also able to develop and encourage an open discourse regarding poverty and the importance of helping the young people of the district learn skills which would help them rise above their poverty.

## Stop and Consider

1. What might the consequences have been if the superintendent had chosen *flight*?
2. What might the consequences have been if the superintendent had chosen *fight*?
3. What other strategies might be implemented to bring this cultural conflict to resolution?

Now go back to the FACC and consider step 4: What might this superintendent do to help individuals involved in this case and others in the district at different locations on the Cultural Highway do to reach Cultural Community?

While the leader and some faculty members may be at Cultural Community, clearly other faculty, administrators, and stakeholders might be at any of the other destinations on the road to Cultural Community. Leaders who acknowledge this likelihood know the importance of continuing the dialogue to reach the goal of Cultural Community. The following are suggestions for leaders to consider as they seek to guide their campus to Cultural Community:

## Activity 1

Engage faculty in once again considering the twelve cultural markers (race, ethnicity/nationality, social class, sex/gender, health, age, geographic region, sexuality, religion, social status, language, and ability/disability). Ask them to reflect on how each of these attributes of culture has influenced their personal and professional lives. How have these cultural experiences affected their own learning and teaching? Having identified these influences, what can educators do to move beyond a focus on the differences to an emphasis on identifying and meeting the needs of all learners on the campus?

## Activity 2

This activity is called "Diversity Dialogue" (Withers & Lewis, 2003, pp. 157–62). Set up tables with a label for each of the twelve cultural groups. Ask individuals to go to the table with which they may identify. Those at that table engage in a conversation for ten to fifteen minutes about what it means to belong to that cultural group. A reporter takes notes to remember important points in the dialogues. Then ask everyone but the reporter to move to another table.

At this next table, the reporter shares what the last group said about what it means to belong to that group. This continues until everyone has visited every table. Then, bring everyone together and ask the following questions: What does it mean to you to be in this large group with us all today? How does it affect you personally and professionally? How does what we are learning about others affect our community as a whole?

## Stop and Consider

What other suggestions would you make to support the superintendent who is committed to leading all stakeholders in his district to arrive at Cultural Community?

## SUMMARY

This chapter has discussed the location of Cultural Community, which emphasizes that everyone is a valued member of the community. When this becomes a goal of everyone on the faculty, it also improves the opportunity to resolve conflicts because communication is open and respectful even when there is disagreement.

## Key Thought

At Cultural Community, leaders focus on a basic respect for shared humanity. However, conflicts will still occur.

## REFLECTION ACTIVITIES

1. As you critically reflect on your own personal development, in relation to what issues are you most likely to be at Cultural Community?
2. What strategies can you identify that helped you move to this point on the cultural highway?
3. Describe an example of a conflict on your campus, even though many are already at Cultural Community.
4. What would you do to resolve the conflict?

*Chapter Ten*

# Are We There Yet?

If we are to achieve a richer culture, rich in contrasting values, we must recognize the whole gamut of human potentialities, and so weave a less arbitrary social fabric, one in which each diverse human gift will find a fitting place.

—Margaret Mead

This book is based on the premise that because much of what educational leaders do happens within a cultural context, it is important to consider the cultural nature of conflicts before resolution can be reached. Whether the school conflict is rooted in the diverse ages of the faculty, the culture of athletics versus that of academics, the culture of individuals from different ethnicities, the culture of poverty versus the culture of middle-income individuals, or another issue, cultural understandings become part of the appropriate resolution.

Utsey, Ponterotto, and Porter (2008) acknowledge that racism, prejudice, and discrimination of all kinds exist in schools and in our communities and contribute to cultural conflict. Yet they also emphasize that the more individuals interact with others from different cultural backgrounds and frameworks, the more harmony and understanding occur. While interaction with diverse populations is an optimal component of handling and understanding cultural conflict (Lindsey, Nuri Robins, & Terrell, 2010), school leaders who nurture covenant communities can focus dialogue and implement conflict strategies that contribute to building cultural community.

The preface to this book discussed some of the many demographic changes that are occurring in our schools, such as the changing student population. However, there are other demographic changes. English, Papa, Mullen, and Creighton (2012) report that poverty in the United States is a growing concern, with rates for African Americans at 25.8 percent and for

Hispanics at 25.3 percent. Additionally, while children are 25 percent of the total population of the nation, they represent 35 percent of the poor population.

The teaching population is also experiencing demographic changes, as Richard Ingersoll (2012) reports. In 1988, there were approximately sixty-five thousand first-year teachers. By 2008, there were over two hundred thousand. In fact, by 2008, 25 percent of teachers had five years or less of experience. At the same time, 40–50 percent of teachers leave teaching within the first five years of their career. While there are certainly many reasons for cultural conflict, there is also no doubt that demographic shifts contribute to conflicts in our schools.

Leaders must understand the different locations on the cultural highway: Cultural Deficit, Cultural Denial, Cultural Discovery, Cultural Celebration, Cultural Conscience, and Cultural Community. This is important in order to establish one's own progress on the cultural highway and to better understand where others are on this journey.

Having a plan to address cultural conflict is important. Thus, the framework for analyzing cultural conflicts (FACC) supports the leader's ability to think strategically through the conflicts in culture that occur on a daily basis at school. Being intentional about identifying the cultural nature of the conflict, choosing whether or not to respond to the conflict and considering possible consequences, and then implementing appropriate conflict resolution strategies supports the leader in leading others toward the goal of Cultural Community.

As covenant relationships are built within the school community, there are increased opportunities for everyone to move forward on the cultural highway. This assumes that transformational moral leaders have a shared goal with their stakeholders, which is to reach Cultural Community. As leaders develop knowledge of each of these locations and discuss inherent conflicts on this journey, they become more comfortable with conflict and thus are able to work toward not only resolving these difficult issues, but moving forward on the cultural highway with greater understanding.

In today's environment of cultural transitions, transformational leaders must facilitate a dialogue that builds on cultural understandings. This dialogue is often difficult, but it is critical to the actions needed for resolution. Thus, educational leaders must get comfortable being uncomfortable. The point of these difficult discussions is not to dwell on differences, but to acknowledge and emphasize that there is a continuum regarding cultural conflict and that all are at different locations at different points in time.

It is a moral imperative for educational leaders to address the cultural continuum in their efforts to bring resolution to conflicts. As theologian Dietrich Bonhoeffer urged, "Not to speak is to speak, not to act is to act."

Without acknowledgment and understanding of the different locations on the cultural highway, one cannot move forward.

Leaders cannot arrive at a place where everyone contributes with equity to the school community without addressing how individuals are different and how individuals are alike, noting their own biases, and then supporting one another to move beyond those biases to achieve community integration. Consequently, the leader's willingness to engage, and knowledge of how to resolve conflicts embedded in cultural issues of race, age, gender, sexual identity, language, social status, and other attributes, can be the catalysts to bring our world together in a sense of community that values our shared humanity.

A famous saying of the baseball great Yogi Berra is that "if you don't know where you are, you're not there yet." Usually this statement is followed by a laugh. But on the more serious side, if leaders don't know where they are on the cultural continuum, or where others are, the chances for conflict are greater. When leaders realize where they are on the cultural continuum and use appropriate conflict resolution skills, educators can negotiate results which build and strengthen relationships among faculty members, students, and other stakeholders in the community.

Having reached Cultural Community on a cultural conflict issue, what is next? Leaders must remember that reaching Cultural Community does not mean that they have arrived at their destination. In fact, the answer to the "Are we there yet?" question is "Probably not." Culture and conflicts are much too complex for there to be a silver bullet that resolves everything.

Achieving Cultural Community does mean, however, that for today, regarding a particular issue, one has made progress that strengthens community. The journey on the cultural highway is an iterative, daily process in which some days are better than others since leaders and stakeholders are at different points of cultural proficiency regarding the various issues. Sometimes there will be agreement; sometimes agreement will be difficult, if not impossible, to reach.

Remember, as you work toward Cultural Community in your journey as leader, that each individual represents a myriad of cultures. If you ask people to describe themselves, generally their descriptions are cultural in nature. For example, someone might identify himself by saying: I'm a leader, a male, a brother, a son, a father, an uncle, a college graduate, Baptist, Hispanic, heterosexual, fortyish, an English speaker, middle income, an amateur basketball player, tall, a dancer, kind . . . and so on. Most of these descriptors are cultural in nature. The various cultures influence how one sees the world and how one responds to that world.

Conflicts arise and they will continue to arise—because no one has the same cultural experiences. No one is like you. Yet everyone is like you. The focus of reaching Cultural Community is that when conflicts occur, the leader has the skills and the strength to encourage and support this diverse group of unalike, alike people in their efforts to work toward resolution.

At Cultural Community, courageous leaders seek those areas where there are common interests and common perspectives so that all can work together toward the common good. Rabindranath Tagore, the first Asian poet to be awarded the Nobel Prize for Literature, encouraged us to "reach high, for stars lie hidden in you. Dream deep, for every dream precedes the goal." Committing to the journey to reach Cultural Community is indeed a worthy goal.

# Appendix 1

*Form for Framework for Analyzing Cultural Conflict*

1. What is the conflict and what is the cultural nature of the conflict?

   a. race
   b. ethnicity/nationality
   c. social class
   d. sex/gender
   e. health
   f. age
   g. geographic region
   h. sexuality
   i. religion
   j. social status
   k. language
   l. ability/disability
   m. other cultural issues

2. What choice will you make at this point in time? *Flight*, *fight*, or *fix* and what are the possible consequences?
3. What conflict strategies will you implement?
4. What activities will you implement in your commitment to continuing on to Cultural Community?

# Appendix 2

## *Mediator Report*

1. "Hi, we will be your mediators today." (Introduce yourselves.)

    Mediator 1: _____ Mediator 2: _____

2. "Please introduce yourselves" (parties in the conflict; may be more than two but all must agree to follow the process). (May wish to shake hands.)

3. Explain the purpose of mediation:

    "We are not here to judge who is guilty or not, or who is right or wrong."
    "We are here to listen and help you solve this conflict."

4. "Before we begin, we need everyone to agree to the following ground rules" (each person must agree to each rule, one at a time—place an X when you look at each person, ask them to agree, and wait for an affirmation—YES—and then thank each person for agreeing to follow the rules):

    Remain seated _____ No put-downs or intentional insults _____
    Do not interrupt _____ Agree to try to solve the problem _____
    Be honest _____ Keep it confidential _____

5. "These are the steps in mediation that we will follow":

You will each have an opportunity to tell your side of the conflict—what happened?

We will make sure that everyone understands the conflict, and that each person understands each other person's point of view.

We will ask you to imagine the conflict from the other person's point of view.

We will ask you to brainstorm suggestions on how to solve the conflict.

If we can reach an agreement to resolve the conflict, you will be asked to sign a contract promising to keep your word and follow the agreement.
If an agreement cannot be reached, the matter will be referred to other sources of authority to address the conflict.

6. "Who would like to go first, and tell us what happened? Remember, everyone will get a chance to tell his or her side." (Make eye contact with each person, listen and repeat the story back to each person—for example, "So I hear you saying . . ." or "In other words, you're saying . . .")

After each person's side is repeated, ask each person if he or she has anything else to add, and, once again, restate or repeat each person's additional comments, making sure that their respective stories have been told and affirmed. Please identify any feelings that are clearly expressed; for example, "So you're saying this happened . . . and you are feeling angry about what happened," or "Because of what you think happened, you are feeling frustrated, stressed, etc."

7. Role reversal—Ask each person to pretend that he or she is in the other person's place, and ask each party to tell how he or she would feel in the other person's shoes. For example, "If you were in her place, and this happened, how would you feel?"

Summarize the feelings of each person based on the role reversal. For example, "So if you were in her shoes and someone accused you of lying when you claim you did not say anything, you would be angry also."

8. Brainstorm solutions—Look at each person and ask, "What can *you* do to try to resolve the conflict?" If one party insists on saying, "He needs to . . ." as a solution, remind him or her that you will ask the other party for solutions next, but right now repeat, "What can *you* do to try to resolve the conflict?" List or describe the solutions/suggestions offered:

      Person no. 1's suggestions: _____

Person no. 2's suggestions: _____

9. Successful solutions—After each person has brainstormed suggestions to resolve the conflict, review each suggestion with each person and ask if he or she agrees with the suggestion. Please mark or note any suggestions that both sides agree to follow.

10. Workable contract—Review all areas of agreement, and then ask each person if he or she believes the agreement will work. Ask: "Will this agreement work? Can you follow this contract?" Then complete the following:

Person no. 1 agrees to: _____
Person no. 2 agrees to: _____

11. Closing—Have each person read what he or she agrees to do, and ask if each has any questions about the agreement. If no questions are asked, or once questions are answered to each person's satisfaction, then have each person sign the contract below:

Person no. 1: _____ Person no. 2: _____
Mediator no. 1: _____ Mediator no. 2: _____

Mediations are often conducted by one mediator, a campus or workplace leader, but many campuses have trained faculty to serve as mediators, and two mediators can often give greater attention to various points in the process. For example, mediators can share responsibility for following the process: Mediator no. 1 could do the odd-numbered items, Mediator no. 2 could do the even-numbered items, and as the one mediator talks, the other mediator can write responses to the respective items.

# Appendix 3

*I Activity*

I feel (describe feeling) when (describe behavior that is disturbing or disruptive) because (state desirable goal or outcome).

I feel _____ when _____ because _____ .

# Appendix 4

## *Equity Audit*

1. Identify issues of systemic inequity within the school and district.
2. Areas of possible review include the three key equity issues: teacher quality (teacher certification, teacher education, teacher experience), program (special education, gifted and talented, bilingual, student discipline), and achievement (state testing results, dropout rates, graduation tracks, SAT results).
3. Analyze to explore why the inequity might be occurring.
4. Identify additional data that need to be collected and assessed.
5. Collaboratively create a preliminary action plan that includes, for example, parents, administrators, school board members, teachers, or superintendent and central office staff members.
6. Make a clear and concise presentation to the faculty and school leadership.
7. Implement plan.
8. Monitor.

## SOURCES

Harris, S., & Hopson, M. (2008). Using equity audits to investigate K–16 campus practices. *Teacher Development, 12*(4), 341–352.

Skrla, L., McKenzie, K., & Scheurich, J. (2009). *Using equity audits to create equitable and excellent schools*. Thousand Oaks, CA: Corwin.

# References

Bagin, D., & Gallagher, D. (2001). *The school and community relations* (7th ed.). Boston: Allyn & Bacon.

Bennis, W., & Goldsmith, J. (1997). *Learning to lead: A workbook on becoming a leader* (rev. ed.). Reading, MA: Perseus Books.

Brislin, R. (1993). *Understanding culture's influence on behavior.* New York: Harcourt Brace College Publishers.

CampbellJones, F., CampbellJones, B., & Lindsey, R. (2010). *The cultural proficiency journey.* Thousand Oaks, CA: Corwin.

Cauchon, D., & Overberg, P. (2012, May 17). Minorities are now a majority of births. *USA Today*, p. 1A.

Coopersmith, J. (2009). *Characteristics of public, private and Bureau of Indian Education elementary and secondary school teachers in the United States: Results from the 2007–08 schools and staffing survey* (NCES 2009-324). Washington, DC: National Center for Education Statistics, Institute of Education Sciences, U.S. Department of Education.

Covey, S. (2004). *The 7 habits of highly effective people: Powerful lessons in personal change* (2nd ed.). New York: Free Press.

Cushner, K. (2003). *Human diversity in action* (2nd ed.). Boston: McGraw Hill.

Diller, J. V., & Moule, J. (2005). *Culture competence: A primer for educators.* Belmont, CA: Wadsworth.

English, F. W., Papa, R., Mullen, C. A., & Creighton, T. (2012). *Educational leadership at 2050.* Lanham, MD: Rowman & Littlefield.

Freire, P. (1970). *Pedagogy of the oppressed.* New York: Herder & Herder.

Goldstein, S. B. (1997). The power of stereotypes: A labeling exercise. *Teaching of Psychology, 24*, 256–258.

Goleman, D. (2000). *Working with emotional intelligence.* New York: Random House.

Harris, S., & Hopson, M. (2008). Using equity audits to investigate K–16 campus practices. *Teacher Development, 12*(4), 341–352.

Hoy, W., & Miskel, C. (2001). *Educational administration: Theory, research, and practice* (6th ed.). Boston: McGraw-Hill.

Hutchins, D., Greenfeld, M., Epstein, J., Sanders, M., & Galindo, C. (2012). *Multicultural partnerships: Involve all families.* Larchmont, NY: Eye on Education.

Ingersoll, R. M. (2012, May). Beginning teacher induction: What the data tell us. *Phi Delta Kappan, 93*(8), 47–51.

Keigher, A. (2009). *Characteristics of public, private, and Bureau of Indian Education elementary and secondary schools in the United States: Results from the 2007–08 schools and staffing survey* (NCES 2009-321). Washington, DC: National Center for Education Statistics, Institute of Education Sciences, U.S. Department of Education.

Klein, J. (2012). *The bully society: School shootings and the crisis of bullying in America's schools*. New York: NYU Press.

Leithwood, K., & Jantzi, D. (2005). Transformational leadership. In B. Davies (Ed.), *The essentials of school leadership* (pp. 31–43). Thousand Oaks, CA: Corwin.

Lindsey, R. B., Nuri Robins, K., & Terrell, R. D. (2010). *Cultural proficiency: A manual for school leaders* (3rd ed.). Thousand Oaks, CA: Corwin.

Lindsey, D. B., Nuri Robins, K., Terrell, R. D., & Lindsey, R. B. (2011). *Culturally proficient instruction: A guide for people who teach* (3rd ed.). Thousand Oaks, CA: Corwin.

Nieto, S. (2005). *Why we teach*. New York: Teachers College Press.

Oakes, J. (2005). *Keeping track: How schools structure inequality* (2nd ed.). New Haven, CT: Yale University Press.

Pang, V. O. (2005). *Multicultural education: A caring-centered reflective approach* (2nd ed.). Boston, MA: McGraw-Hill.

Purkey, W. (1992). Conflict resolution: An invitational approach. *Journal of Invitational Theory and Practice, 1*(2), 111. www.invitationaleducation.net/publications/journal/v12p111.htm.

Quantz, R. A. (2007). Rethinking systems and conflict in schools. In D. Carlson & C. P. Gause (Eds.), *Keeping the promise: Essays on leadership, democracy, and education* (pp. 46–60). New York: Peter Lang.

Scharrer, G., & Lacoste-Caputo, J. (2010, May 16). State's future is here. *San Antonio Express-News*, pp. 1A, 14A–15A.

Sergiovanni, T. (1996). *Leadership for the schoolhouse*. San Francisco: Jossey-Bass.

Singleton, G., & Linton, C. (2006). *Courageous conversations about race: A field guide for achieving equity in schools*. Thousand Oaks, CA: Corwin.

Skrla, L., McKenzie, K., & Scheurich, J. (2009). *Using equity audits to create equitable and excellent schools*. Thousand Oaks, CA: Corwin.

Thomas, K. (1976). Conflict and conflict management. In M. D. Dunnette (Ed.), *Handbook of industrial and organizational psychology* (pp. 889–936). Chicago: Rand McNally.

Tyson, K. (2011). *Integration interrupted: Tracking, black students, and acting white after Brown*. New York: Oxford University Press.

Utsey, S. O., Ponterotto, J. G., & Porter, J. S. (2008). Prejudice and racism, year 2008—still going strong: Research on reducing prejudice with recommended methodological advances. *American Counseling Association, 86*, 339–347.

Valenzuela, A. (1999). *Subtractive schooling: US-Mexican youth and the politics of caring*. Albany: State University of New York Press.

Whitaker, T. (2012). *What great teachers do differently: 17 things that matter most* (2nd ed.). Larchmont, NY: Eye on Education.

Withers, B., & Lewis, K. D. (2003). *The conflict and communication activity book*. New York: AMACOM.

# About the Authors

**Sandra Harris** received her PhD from the University of Texas at Austin. She is currently professor and dissertation coordinator for the Center for Research and Doctoral Studies in Educational Leadership at Lamar University in Beaumont, Texas. Formerly she served as a teacher, principal, and superintendent in public and private schools. Her scholarship agenda includes leadership and building relationship-oriented, socially just school environments. She specializes in qualitative research and social justice issues. She is the author of over one hundred journal articles and book chapters. In addition, she has authored or co-authored twenty-one books on a variety of topics that emphasize leadership in public and private schools. Dr. Harris presents at regional, state, and national conferences on these and other related topics.

**Steve Jenkins** received his Doctor of Education degree from Baylor University. He is currently associate professor in the Department of Educational Leadership at Lamar University. Dr. Jenkins has spent more than thirty-five years working in public schools as a teacher, campus administrator, and central office administrator. He has also served as a conflict management specialist in a state education agency, an executive director of a national research and development center, and a university professor. Dr. Jenkins's experience also includes nearly a decade working as a teacher and administrator in a large inner-city school district, as well as working with smaller school districts as an administrator with a state education agency. He has had several texts and articles published in the areas of civil and educational rights, school law, cultural proficiency, conflict resolution, and inclusion.

www.ingramcontent.com/pod-product-compliance
Lightning Source LLC
Chambersburg PA
CBHW080243270326
41926CB00020B/4354